DATE DUE

DEMCO 38-296

STUDIES IN

AFRICAN AMERICAN HISTORY AND CULTURE

edited by

GRAHAM RUSSELL HODGES
COLGATE UNIVERSITY

A GARLAND SERIES

Dr. Barbara Ann Teer
(Photograph by Bernard Fairclough)

BARBARA ANN TEER AND THE NATIONAL BLACK THEATRE

Transformational Forces in Harlem

LUNDEANA MARIE THOMAS

GARLAND PUBLISHING, Inc.
New York & London / 1997

ng-in-Publication Data

Thomas, Lundeana Marie, 1949–
  Barbara Ann Teer and the National Black Theatre :
transformational forces in Harlem / Lundeana Marie Thomas.
      p.   cm. — (Studies in African American history and
culture)
  Revision of the author's thesis (Ph. D.)—University of
Michigan, 1993.
  Includes bibliographical references and index.
  ISBN 0-8153-2920-2 (alk. paper)
  1. National Black Theatre (New York, N.Y.)—History.
2. Theater—New York (State)—New York—History—20th
century. 3. Afro-American theater—New York (State)—New
York—History—20th century. 4. Teer, Barbara Ann. I. Title.
II. Series.
PN2297.N28T56 1997
792'.089'9607471—dc21   97-16332

Printed on acid-free, 250-year-life paper
Manufactured in the United States of America

To Mom, Dad, Bernard, John Mark, and LeeRoy

Contents

List of Illustrations

List of Appendices

Foreword

For nearly thirty years the National Black Theatre and the name of its founder, Barbara Ann Teer, have been spoken in "the same breath." Unknown to most readers, however, are the intimate details of how Teer, an accomplished actress, dancer, author, educator and producer became disillusioned with "The Great White way," decided to go "back home" to Harlem, to create a "soul theatre," and to change the perception of American theatre, especially Black Theatre. The pieces of this fascinating story finally come together in this volume. The saga begins with a historical overview of carefully chosen facts that prepares us for the coming of Teer. The reader is then given a penetrating look at Teer's early background, her training and experiences in the American theatre of the 1950s and 60s. Then a sensitive and profusely documented tour of Teer's move back home to Harlem begins. The evolution of her philosophy, theories, practices and aspirations unfolds in the pages that follow. We come to understand that the theatre Teer sought to create in 1968 was not militant; the transformation she sought was spiritual, not social. The revolution she envisioned would take place in the hearts and minds of Blacks. Teer's continuing search for this spiritual truth in the Yoruba rituals of Nigeria, in the Pentecostal Church and in the Harlem community helps us to grasp the driving spirit or "soul," if you will, of this remarkable woman. The development of The National Black Theatre is revealed simultaneously. The edifice that occupies a block on 125th Street, Teer's pragmatic place for shedding the ills of cultural hegemony, stands today as a monument to her continuing efforts to transform a community.

Thomas' close relationship; with Teer and NBT, her first-hand acquaintance with Pentecostalism, her own beliefs in the values of a pluralistic society and of the use of positive energy to effect change, all add credibility to the writing. Clearly, Teer's determination to build NBT on "what might be, what is possible, what's missing and what can be provided" is heard here by the writer. It is the underpinning of both Teer's and Thomas' efforts and provides us with a substantial base on which to view Teer as a builder of the community and of the "quintessential black theatre of Harlem."

Dr. Winona L. Fletcher
Indiana University
Professor Emeritus
Theatre and Drama and Afro-American Studies

Acknowledgments

I wish to thank Barbara Ann Teer for having the vision, courage, fortitude, and determination to create a National Black Theatre. Many thanks to the National Black Theatre family who nurtured it during its years of growth and were so helpful in supplying materials for the completion of this work. They include: Abisola, Adunni, Ade, Nabii, Tunde, Reena, and Denyse.

I am grateful to my family and friends for their patience, love, and understanding during the preparation of this manuscript. This especially includes: Mr. LeeRoy and Rev. Mercy Dea Thomas, John Mark, LeeRoy, Edmond Ward, Anne Fannin, Julius P. Lundy, Sr., Renee Simmons, Robin Means-Coleman, and Lorna Littleway.

I humbly thank Rev. Katie Nugent and Sis. Virginia Blueford who always include me in their prayers. A special homage to my ancestors: Grandmother, Elizabeth Gilford; Great-Aunt, Aunt Willie Bee; "Special Friend," Estelle Revish, and "Aunt Viv,"Vivian Robinson, thanks for your love and guidance.

I must gratefully acknowledge the members of Saint Matthew Fire Baptized Holiness Church of God of the Americas. Thank you for your prayers, songs, and testimonies of encouragement.

A special thanks to Dr. Winona L. Fletcher for her contribution to this work and so many other gifts. God knows I could not have completed this or other projects without her assistance, wisdom, and love.

I wish to thank Dr. Leigh Woods of the University of Michigan for his tutelage and Dr. Thomas Copeland of Youngstown State University, whose expertise and support were invaluable. Thanks also to Gwendolyn Ricks-Spencer who first acquainted me with the National Black

Theatre and to Dr. Mark Pilkinton who encouraged me to research it further.

To those who helped with this manuscript—a big "Thanks" to Darnell L. Johnson, Bernard Thomas, Mah'Gee Foster, David Baugh, and The University of Louisville. Many thanks to those who answered my questionnaires and allowed themselves to be interviewed including Woodie King, Jr., Vivian Robinson, James Pringle, James V. Hatch, and Amiri Baraka.

I wish to express my sincere gratitude to Dr. Graham Hodges and Garland Publishing for the African American History and Culture Series. Kudos to my Editor, Kristi Long, and computer specialist, Chuck Bartelt, for their help and special assistance.

And more than all I thank GOD.

Introduction

In 1965 noted African-American[1] poet and playwright Langston Hughes perceived "a very great need for a serious theatre in the Harlem Community . . . a theatre in which the drama and the folk arts of the Negro people might be presented before the very audiences out of whom this drama is born."[2] He was not the first to recognize this need. According to James Hatch,

> In 1926, W. E. B. DuBois supervised the formation of the Krigwas, a theatre that was to produce plays *about* Negroes, *by* Negroes, *for* Negroes and *near* Negroes. In 1965, LeRoi Jones demanded a theatre *about* black people, *with* black people, *for* black people, and *only* black people.[3]

Nor would their voices be heard as the last or the most vociferous, for Ed Bullins also called for a National Black Theatre in Harlem, to serve as "a medium for communication to raise the consciousness throughout the nation, for black artistic, political, and cultural consciousness. And it would be an institution for the black people in America who are a nation within a nation."[4]

In 1968, one charismatic Black female accepted Hughes' challenge. Broadway actress Barbara Ann Teer burst upon the scene advocating "the creation of a black theory of acting and liberating."[5]

Her proposal moved Hughes' vision beyond just "a serious Harlem theatre" to a holistic training program from which would emerge new productions and new performers, in a permanent home that would perpetuate an African-American theatre ideologically and financially separate from those of the White majority.

Both Hughes and Teer knew a kind of theatre based on traditions and standards known most recently as "Western" or "Euro-American" or "Eurocentric," or just simply as "Caucasian" or "White." Both knew that the origin of theatre was a controversial subject and that, according to theatre historian Oscar Brockett, the evolution of theatre "can be constructed by the historian only by guesswork. Therefore, it is not surprising that many theories about the origin of the theatre have been advanced and that none can be verified."[6] They also knew, along with other Blacks, that Western theatre as an art form grew out of traditions embedded in early Greek culture, denying any African influence. The African-American theatre wanting to embrace African influence has had to struggle against traditions and standards well established by the dominant culture to discover and create its own unique roots from the theatrical activities of Africa. Many African-Americans yearned to investigate and communicate to the world their link to Africa. "Because Afro-American theatre stems from roots on both sides of a hyphen," writes Hatch, "the hyphen must become a bridge"[7] in order to pass on the heritage through rituals, stories, and "Africanisms" that distinguish Afro-American theatre from Euro-American rituals and traditions.

Both Hughes and Teer made this discovery the hard way—by trying first to meet White expectations and standards of evaluation. Both Hughes' attempt in the 1930s, and Teer's in the early 1960s, left them convinced that success in such an endeavor was inconsistent with a feeling of fulfillment as an artist. Such discontent with theatrical traditions was not confined to the Black artistic community, but it had more revolutionary consequences because it was joined with other forms of social unrest.

For Whites the break with tradition in the decades between 1950 and 1980 meant breaking with "the conservative, conventional, elitist, realistic, well-tried" theories and practices and moving toward "the experimental, the populist, the non-realistic, the political, and the activist"[8] theatre. Hence, there arose such theatres as Richard

Schechner's Environmental Theatre, the Open Theatre, Grotowski's Poor Theatre, LaMama Experimental Theatre, the Living Theatre, the Polish Laboratory Theatre, and the El Teatro Campesino. It was no coincidence that these experimental theatres arose concurrently with the movement away from Broadway to off-Broadway and off-off Broadway in New York City. Broadway meant commercialization and conformity, and it stood antithetical to the aims of the theatres that broke with "tradition."[9]

For Blacks the break with tradition meant doing something entirely different from what Whites were doing. "Tradition," for Hughes and Teer, was synonymous with "White" and encompassed any and all forms and styles of theatre that were conceived and controlled by Whites. Breaking with tradition for African-Americans meant searching for relevancy in theatre from among their own traditions that sprang from their African heritage. Above all, it meant rejecting White-controlled theatres after many years of "trying to fit in." In short, it meant facing the reality of society's unfulfilled promises of assimilation and integration. Ed Bullins declared,

> We don't want to have a higher form of white art in Black faces. We are working toward something entirely different and new that encompasses the soul and spirit of Black people, and that represents the whole experience of our being here in this oppressive land. . . . (Anything less than this is UNREAL).[10]

Not all Blacks felt as strongly as Bullins, but most Blacks knew by the late 1960s that it was time to reclaim their own identity through the raising of Black consciousness, and many worked to accomplish this task.

Despite differences between Black and White conceptions of and motivations for breaking with "tradition," even a cursory examination of the most "experimental" White theatres that came to be known as "experimental" will reveal some rather obvious similarities to comparable Black theatres. First, there were the populist-oriented, communal, and ritual experiences practiced by many experimental theatres of the 1960s. These theatres often used improvisation, interaction with audiences, rebellion against many elements of realism, re-defining of theatrical space, renouncing the importance of the text, and shifting emphasis from "product" to "process." While there were efforts toward racial integration in some experimental groups, these failed for three basic reasons: blindness to the differences between Black and White cultures, failure to address these differences in a positive manner and setting, and the lack of Black control or influence over the communication of these differences. Barbara Ann Teer had notions about how to reconcile many experimental theatre ideas with the Black experience and so bring validation to a group suffering from the negative effects of cultural hegemony. She shared the pain felt by many Blacks of the 1960s, but she refused to let it turn into hate as many others did. She felt that this negativism would destroy Black hope. Instead she sought to turn this spiritual and emotional energy into positive action. Teer's ideas eventually found expression through the formation of the National Black Theatre in 1968.

Teer sought a theatre in Harlem based on combining the dual heritage of being African and American by embracing theatre's oldest form of ritual, religion. As Greek drama began with the rituals honoring the god Dionysus, Teer began a theatre to honor God and his creation of African-Americans. Teer's idea was to combine elements of the Black Pentecostal worship services and the religious and ceremonial rites of the Yoruba tribe from Nigeria, Africa. Her initial motivation came in the belief that this combination would yield a theatre which could, in her words,

> Be used as a tool to create a wider communication—Black people with Black people—to attempt to reverse the process of negative thinking that has been entrenched within our people and replace it with positive thoughts through the process of self-examination.[11]

The NBT, again in Teer's words "employs in its performances—the belief that acting is a study of life and that Black life throughout American history has evolved through five distinct stages: [the] nigger, negro, militant, nationalist, [and] revolutionary."[12] It was Teer's hope that through a revolutionary spirit and a communal celebration of self the African-American could finally escape from the ill-effects of cultural hegemony.

Thus, Teer and the NBT are worthy of extensive study for several reasons. The theatre has broken new ground in creating an African-American theory of acting. It developed training utilizing African-American cultural traditions rather than following Eurocentric traditions. While other theatres have come and gone, the NBT is still thriving as one of the oldest African-American theatres in the country, and the very oldest experimental theatre in Harlem. It continues to produce African-American theatre for a predominantly African-American audience. It also continues to provide a venue for African-American writers, a training ground for African-American artists, and an example of African-American entrepreneurial success. In 1989, the *Philadelphia Tribune* paid tribute to the NBT:

> In 1970 there were over 112 Black Theatre Companies operating in the New York City area. Today [1989] there are less than 10 full-time theaters. [The] National Black Theatre is one of those 10 theater companies and is considered to be one of the cultural treasurers of this decade.[13]

A still more striking tribute was paid in 1986, with the awarding of a National Endowment for the Arts Challenge Grant to the NBT. President Ronald Reagan proclaimed that "the National Black Theatre is a cultural treasure. It is one of the 63 most important art institutions in America."[14] In 1990 the NBT celebrated the grand opening of its new $12 million building, which made the NBT "the only Black Theatre Organization in New York City to own a city block of property."[15]

As part of this grand opening celebration, the theatre created a press packet which included a list of those who had studied with Barbara Ann Teer and the NBT training program:

> Obba Babatunde (star of "Dream Girls"); Avery Brooks (TV star, "A Man Called Hawk" & "Spenser for Hire"); Antonio Fargas (movie, TV and stage star); Clarice Taylor (Cliff Huxtable's mother on "The Cosby Show"); and Hattie Winston (movie, TV and stage star); and, arts administrators such as: Duane Jones (deceased) of the Richard

Allen Cultural Center for the Arts and Zuri McKie, Director, Theatre Program, NYS Council on the Arts; were trained at NBT.[16]

This list gives some indication of the impact that the NBT has had and continues to have on entertainment in America.

The purpose of this book is to trace the development of the National Black Theatre under the artistic direction of Barbara Ann Teer. Accordingly, I will examine the objectives, training, texts, and practices of the NBT in order to ascertain the contribution of this company to African-American theatre, to theatre in America, and to the African-American community. Because this is the first major study of the National Black Theatre, attention is given to the philosophy which precipitated the theory and practice of this organization. In addition to providing historical background, this study focuses on Teer's effort to develop for an American audience a uniquely African-American theatrical art form, and it attempts to ascertain the impact of this art form on the theatrical profession in general and on Black theatre in particular.

This study records the theory and techniques of the National Black Theatre in Teer's attempt to create a new form of artistic expression and to teach it to her company. This study also examines the viability and practicality of this new form for other theatre companies and educational theatres. It also inquires into the source of the longevity of the NBT as the longest-lived experimental theatre in Harlem. By focusing on an African-American female artistic director, this study also contributes to research on women and minorities in the arts.

Books on African-American theatre history which mention the NBT at all list it as an experimental theatre of the 1960s, but they provide only fragmentary information about its early history and do not examine its development since the 1970s. Books offering general coverage of experimental theatres of the 1960s do not include the National Black Theatre, despite its similarity to other experimental theatres.

In *Black Theater in America*, James Haskins gives an overview of the history of African-American theatre from the nineteenth century to the present. He identifies the NBT as an experimental group that stresses collective rather than individual effort, and he briefly outlines the NBT's goals and details their practices. However, he does not discuss the theatre's artistic vision or how this vision has been implemented. Haskins mentions the group's use of "rituals" but does not outline what they are or how they are performed.

Genevieve Fabre, in *Drumbeats, Masks, and Metaphor*, chronicles contemporary Black theatre from 1945 to the present. She mentions the NBT along with other Black theatres which used ritual as the basis of their theatrical performances, but she gives more detailed information about the theatres of Ed Bullins and Amiri Baraka than about the NBT. Fabre also writes about the NBT's combination of African and American traditions, and she regards Yoruba ritual as similar to the rituals used by a number of Black theatre companies. I will explore this similarity in greater detail in Chapter IV.

Mance Williams, in *Black Theatre in the 1960s and 1970s: A Historical-Critical Analysis of the Movement*, considers Teer and the NBT more extensively than do Haskins or Fabre. Williams asserts that the NBT is involved in establishing a God-conscious art, but he does not explain what that means. He offers information about Teer's ritualistic revivals as performances, but he offers no critical analysis of them.

The Theatre of Black Americans, edited by Errol Hill, contains an article written by Jessica Harris highlighting NBT's goals and objectives, and a synopsis of one of the company's ritualistic revivals. But once again, Harris merely lists the theatre's goals without examining their significance. Harris quotes Teer's statement that the NBT intends to create a new art form, but she does not define that form or explain its difference from Eurocentric theatre.

Karen Malpede, in *Women in Theatre: Compassion and Hope*, is the only female writer to publish a lengthy interview with Teer. *Women in American Theatre*, edited by Helen Krich Chinoy and Linda Walsh Jenkins, merely reprints Malpede's interview.

Articles about Teer or the NBT have appeared in the *New York Times*, *Essence*, *Ebony*, *People*, and many other magazines and newspapers. The NBT and Teer are listed in African-American periodicals dating from 1970 to the present, and they are also included in Bernard Peterson's *Contemporary Black American Playwrights and Their Plays: A Biographical Directory and Dramatic Index*. The present study is the first to deal with the journalistic treatments of the NBT.

I have used a combination of procedures in this study. Primary sources include personal interviews with Teer, with members of the NBT company, and with some of those who have registered in classes or viewed performances. Most of the secondary sources concerning the NBT are housed in the theatre's office, at the Schomburg Library in Harlem, the Hatch-Billops Collection, and in the New York Public Library at Lincoln Center. Secondly, I have used reviews of the NBT's "ritualistic revivals" to summarize the plots of these events and to suggest the reactions of the critics. Thirdly, in order to detail the NBT's training, I have supplemented my interviews with Teer, NBT members, and applicants to the NBT classes with personal observations of several class sessions. Finally, I used an analytical approach to evaluate the theatre's differences from theatres governed by Eurocentric standards and practices. Such comparisons will help to show to what extent Teer has accomplished what she intended for her theatre and what impact she has had on Black theatre in Harlem and the United States as a whole.

Chapter I is an overview of African-American theatre history that suggests why Teer founded her theatre as an alternative for Blacks who remained "outside" the White theatres of the 1960s. Chapter II provides a biographical sketch of Teer and examines the basis of her approach to theatre in African and Pentecostal ritual worship. Teer's first steps in building upon this foundation—the formation of her theatre and the articulation of its philosophy—are the subjects of Chapter III. This leads in turn to Chapter IV's study of the practical working-out of these goals in training practices, classes, and exercises. Chapter IV also compares Teer's methods of training actors with more commonly accepted actor-training methods. Chapter V evaluates the NBT as a whole, analyzing selected performances, critical responses, and the social impact of the NBT as a cultural institution. The Conclusions provide a final assessment of the theatre and its contributions to the Harlem community.

From the NBT's inception until 1983, Teer was the company's artistic director and executive producer. After a fire in 1983, Teer believed that the NBT needed a permanent theatre. She turned her artistic duties over to members of the NBT in order to plan and raise money for a new theatre complex; she has since taught classes only when her schedule permits.

In 1990 her long-term goal became a reality, in the form of a theatre complex bearing a new name: The National Black Theatre's Institute of Action Arts. Because of the magnitude of this change, this study will not include detailed information of the NBT's re-structuring or of the modifications NBT has since made in its goals. Instead, I will concentrate on the NBT's beginning, its philosophy, its differences from White-oriented theatre, and its impact on theatre and the African-American community in Harlem.

NOTES

1. "Black," "Negro," "Afro-American," and "African-American" are equivalent terms representing a group of Americans of African descent as characterized by dark complexion. The terms are used as each contributor has used them. When "Black" or "Blacks" is used to mean Negro it can be capitalized. Likewise "White," being substituted for "Caucasian," can be capitalized. See Lynn Quitman Troyka, *The Simon and Shuster Handbook for Writers*, 3rd ed. (Englewood Cliffs, N.J.: Prentice-Hall, Inc., 1993), 30e, p. 535.

2. Langston Hughes, "The Need for an Afro-American Theatre," *The International Library of Negro Life and History-Anthology of the American Negro in the Theatre*, 2nd ed., ed. Lindsay Patterson (New York: Publisher's Company, Inc., 1969), p. 163.

3. James V. Hatch, *Black Theatre U.S.A.* (New York: The Free Press, 1974), p. 773.

4. Marvin X, "An Interview with Ed Bullins: Black Theatre," *Negro Digest* 18 (April 1969), 12-13.

5. Jessica B. Harris, "The National Black Theatre: The Sun People of 125th Street," *The Theatre of Black Americans,* ed. Errol Hill (New York: Applause, 1980, 1987), p. 285.

6. Oscar Brockett, *History of the Theatre*, 2nd ed. (Boston: Allyn and Bacon, Inc., 1974), p. 2.

7. Hatch, "Here Comes Everybody: Scholarship and Black Theatre History," *Interpreting the Theatrical Past: Essays in Historiography of Performance*, ed. Thomas Postlewait and Bruce McConachie (Iowa City: University of Iowa press, 1989), p. 150.

8. Joseph Papp, Introduction, *New York's Other Theatre: A Guide to Off Off Broadway*, by Mindy N. Levine (New York: Avon Books, 1981), pp. xi-xvii.

9. Papp, p. xi-xvii.

10. Marvin X, p. xii.

11. Quoted in Larry Bivins, "Success Without Compromise," *Newsday* 14 April 1988, p. 24.

12. Bivins, p. 24.

13. "Black Theatre Breaks Ground," *The Philadelphia Tribune* May 16, 1989, p. C-1.

14. "Black Theatre Breaks Ground," p. C-1.

15. "Black Theatre Breaks Ground," p. C-1.

16. Facts Sheet, National Black Theatre's Healing Hands across Harlem, November 1, 1990, p. 7.

Barbara Ann Teer and the National Black Theatre

I
Before the National Black Theatre

The conflicts inherent in being African-American artists in the world of traditional American theatre led to the development of what was to be called the Black Arts Movement. This movement, that rejected the need to create a theatre in the image of the dominant White culture, was a stimulus for the establishment of the National Black Theatre [NBT]. Before founding the NBT of Harlem in 1968, Barbara Ann Teer was enjoying success as an actress on the Broadway stage. The reasons for her transformation from an actress of Western traditional theatre to the director of a Black theatre are complex. A better understanding of Teer's theatre can be achieved by first examining the history of African-American theatre before 1968. Because theatre has always been a reflection of life, this investigation will necessitate an examination of the lives of African-Americans as they were reflected in the world of the American theatre.

This chapter focuses on the African cultural heritage of African-Americans, which is rooted in rich theatrical conventions. Black art was suppressed by slave holders and parodied by the nineteenth-century theatrical producers into ugly, demeaning stereotypes. African-American writers and performers were forced by White-dominated theatre to perpetuate these stereotypes on stage or to work outside of the American theatre. Occasional accomplishments by Black performers led to projects modeled upon Eurocentric dramatic structure, espoused the moral values of the dominant majority, and benefited White producers. Black intellectuals from as early as the

1920s called for the creation of a truly Black theatre that was produced by and for African-Americans, that celebrated their cultural heritage, and that addressed the concerns of the Black community. However, it was not until the Black Power Movement, arising from the civil rights struggle of the 1950s and 1960s, that Black playwrights began to challenge the Black community with plays that needed a Black theatre—a theatre that was ideologically and financially separate from that of the White majority.

American theatre history, for the African-American, might be seen as an example of "cultural hegemony," a term denoting the almost inevitable result of the coexistence of two or more cultures: one typically subjugates the others or seduces them into conformity. The overt power and the covert glamour of the dominant or "hegemonic" culture constitute its cultural hegemony. Members of the subordinate cultures are said to "assimilate" to the dominant culture, and although they may only grudgingly acquiesce in certain demands, they eagerly comply with others, for, as Bruce McConachie writes, "People will always need to identify with others because of their fear of alienation and estrangement."[1] The theory of cultural hegemony has a direct bearing on understanding the development of Black Theatre in the United States.

Since Western theatre history is grounded in the history of Greek culture, and since theatre in America grew out of Western traditions, African-American theatre has had difficulty establishing its African roots.[2] Black artists have suffered from feelings of inferiority and have expressed shame for those characteristics of speech, music, and dance that linked them to Africa, characteristics that James V. Hatch notes as "Africanisms":

> For Afro-Americans, a shared glory with the Pharaohs is as legitimate as shared glory with the Greeks for Western Caucasians. When Afro-American culture is denied African roots, it is left to attach itself to European traditions which afforded it little respect. Because Afro-American theatre stems from roots on both sides of a hyphen, the hyphen must become a bridge. Africanisms that survived must be investigated—a difficult task which takes the historian into anthropology, sociology, psychology, and religion.[3]

Africanisms are cultural artifacts, like speech, music, and dance that survived the infamous middle passage. Other nationalities often adjusted their names in order to assimilate faster, but with time the stigma attached to the Irish, the Italian, and the Scottish has faded. These ethnic groups were able to assimilate faster because their differences were less easily discernible. However, the darker complexions, kinky hair, and full lips of African-Americans are salient features and are not so readily disguised. African-Americans were taught to be ashamed not only of their physical characteristics but also of many cultural, educational, and social characteristics which made them different. It is this enduring shame at their own heritage that distinguishes African-Americans from all other immigrants to America.

Amiri Baraka[4] defines the African-American or American Negro as a unique race created by the oppressive conditioning of slavery. He also reminds us that people of African descent are the only race who did not happily migrate to the United States looking for freedom of opportunity. Instead, Africans were "brought to this country in bondage and remained so for more than two hundred fifty years. But most of the Black people who were freed from formal slavery in 1863 were not Africans. They were Americans."[5] The indoctrination received by slaves, viewed by many as a form of oppression, had produced a post-Emancipation group of Black people whose familiarity with the mores, attitudes, languages, and other cultural references of this country rivaled those of willing immigrants trying desperately to embrace these same mores by choice. But the much older African heritage has survived at a deeper level, and it is from this source that many modern Blacks derive their sense of identity. African-Americans have preserved a portion of their ancient heritage in the form of Africanisms, a source for much of modern Black drama.

Unlike the Egyptians' written history, which has largely perished, the Black oral tradition has survived, committed not to paper or clay but to the practice and habit of oral history. The offspring of emancipated Negroes learned about Africa and slavery primarily through the stories, tales, riddles, and songs of their older relatives descended from early Africans, of kingdoms like the Benin, the Zulu, the Kikuyu, the Mendi, the Bantu, the Yoruba, and others south of the Sahara.[6] In addition to tales, riddles, and songs, this oral tradition consists of still more pervasive cultural habits (e.g., roughness or sweetness of speech, pitch variations, booming tones, and body language) revealing a speaker's emotional state: "It embraces silent signals locked within the voiced speech as well as an aura of signals," as Hatch describes them, "surrounding the voiced content of the speech";[7] in other words, subtextual language and emotional depth. Collectively these aspects of African oral tradition can be called Africanisms.

Africanisms are still part of the lives of Black people to varying degrees in Haiti, Brazil, Cuba, and Guyana. Baraka explains:

> Africanisms in American Negroes are not now readily discernible, although they certainly do exist. It was in the United States only that the slaves were, after a few generations, unable to retain much of their more obvious African traditions, yet some basic and fundamental traditions endured.[8]

In the United States in particular, the African oral tradition is largely limited to such Africanisms as rituals and tales. These were often harshly suppressed by slavemasters who, fearing the results of allowing slaves a sense of their own history and human dignity, sought to have these Africanisms buried forever. Genevieve Fabre reports that

> The oral tradition holds a prominent place in Afro-American culture. For slaves (who were often forbidden to learn to write) it was the safest means of communication. It provided basic contact with Africa as a homeland and a source of folklore, a contract [sic] also between ethnic groups unified under a common symbolic heritage, between generations, and finally, between the speaker and his audience.[9]

Black slaves were forbidden to practice any African rituals, to speak African dialect, or to communicate anything about the land beyond the "river." Both written and unwritten laws, pre- and post-slavery, forbade the practice of the ways of indigenous African culture. Violation of these laws was punishable by death.[10] However, the less recognizable manifestations of the ancestral culture were tolerated.

Slave narratives contain numerous references to instruments brought from Africa and using African references. Hatch notes that

> The kinds of laughter, the placement of the voice in the throat, gestures of the hands, face, and feet passed and received unconsciously—all provided direct transfusion of Africanisms from parent to child. . . . these signals have transmitted racial memory and, in many examples, specific bonding rituals: "signifying," "rappin'," "toasting," and boasting appear formally on the Black stage and less formally on the street. To hear and enjoy these silences fully, one must either have grown up black or have learned them through study.[11]

The covertness of this survival of Africanisms endowed them with greater emotional power among African-Americans. And since oppression was also suppression of the spirit, the preservation of the African heritage required either a great masking or a hardening of the emotions. Paul Lawrence Dunbar, in "We Wear the Mask," expresses with mournful sensitivity the figurative complexities of masks and masquerading in the lives of African-American people.[12] James Anderson reports that

> In America, as white children leave home and move on through the educational system and then into the work of the world, the development of cognitive and learning styles follows a linear, self-reinforcing course. Never are they asked to be bicultural, bidialectic, or bicognitive. On the other hand, for children of color biculturality is not a free choice, but a prerequisite for successful participation and eventual success. Non-white children generally, are expected to be bicultural, bidialectic, bicognitive; to measure their performance against a Euro-American yardstick; and to maintain the psychic energy to maintain this orientation.[13]

In other words, African-Americans have learned to behave one way at school or with Whites but another way at home or with members of their own culture. This reversion is as important as the adaptation itself, its purpose being to avert ridicule and/or physical abuse by people of their own culture who might resent any appearance of trying to be "better" than they. Therefore, historically, masking and masquerading have been a vital and necessary means of survival for African-Americans among Whites and even among members of their own culture.

Two important points must be clarified before discussing the Black experience in American theatre and its relationship to Barbara Ann Teer and the NBT. First, the image of the Black American was in American theatre long before Blacks themselves became a genuine part of it. Second, the notion of a Black theatre with playwrights, actors, composers, musicians, and technicians, founded primarily to serve the cultural needs of the Black community and to express its life, had a traceable history long before it became a clear possibility.

Stereotypical Black characters in White plays were accepted long before more complex, realistic Black characters were allowed on stage. Although some free Black people lived in the United States before the Civil War, most Blacks were slaves, and each slave was considered "three-fifths of the white man"[14] in the census count until the Emancipation Proclamation of 1863. At that time the theatrical image of the Black was that of partial human being, too. An additional reason for the absence of a fully rounded Black character from the pre-Civil War stage may be that Black roles were played by White actors. According to *The Negro Almanac*,

> Apparently the first black character in an American play appeared in *The Disappointment; or, The Force of Credulity* in 1767. The character, a comic stereotype, was named Raccoon. Comic roles were the forte of the white-turned-black actor.[15]

Other noted White actors who performed in blackface were Edwin Forrest, Lewis Hallam, "Sol" Smith, Bernard Flaherty, and Edwin Booth.

The idea of a Black theatre was slow to emerge and still slower to receive documentation, for Blacks interested in the theatre lacked training and their initial efforts were generally crude by prevailing standards.[16] According to *The Negro Almanac*, "from the earliest days of slavery, entertainment was one of the few avenues of expression open to Blacks." On the other hand,

> For more than a century, the most formidable obstacle faced by the black entertainer was the fact that he was excluded—both as a spectator and participant—from those public places of entertainment which are the logical training ground for any performer.[17]

Thus deprived of proper training, Blacks made little progress toward the establishment of a Black theatre. Many Whites continued to find satisfaction in seeing Blacks as comic characters which they portrayed in blackface.

Most commercial productions did not cast Blacks even in comic roles. Whites in blackface continued to fill these roles not because Blacks were incompetent but because many Whites did not want to associate with Black actors socially or professionally. Not only were Blacks excluded from White commercial theatre but "serious plays of Negro life were generally considered box-office poison," and were not being considered because "few Negroes were among New York's theatre-goers."[18] Such attitudes continued well into the twentieth century.

During the nineteenth century a free Black named Brown (first name uncertain), set out to provide entertainment for patrons who came to his tea garden. In 1821 this semi-professional African Company was founded with funds from his Harlem coffee-house establishment, from which came the name of the theatre, the African Grove. There *The Drama of King Shotaway* was presented, the first recorded play written, produced, and performed by Blacks in America.[19]

Much Black theatre in the early nineteenth century emulated White American theatre, which, in turn, followed European theatrical practices in form, style, and repertory. James Hewlett, Ira Aldridge, and Brown were able to see plays from a special gallery for Blacks at the Park Theatre, and they would later imitate the performances they had witnessed. Accordingly, Shakespearean plays and other classics were presented at the African Grove, interspersed with various comic acts. The African Grove company played mainly to Black audiences, with the back of the house accommodating curious White spectators. Some

Whites had apparently created enough disruption to force the management to seat them in the rear, and a sign was posted in the theatre to explain that Whites did not know "how to behave themselves at entertainments designed for ladies and gentlemen of colour."[20] "The African Grove Theatre," writes Haskins, "represented no more than a small, brief effort on the part of a few idealistic black people to start something for which most black New Yorkers were not ready and that most white New Yorkers were unwilling to allow."[21] The African Grove enjoyed a significant success, but a short one. The theatre was closed in 1822 because of a disturbance by White rioters and, after reopening briefly, was closed again in 1823 when the riots recommenced.[22]

The African Grove was also significant for the introduction of two important actors, James Hewlett and Ira Aldridge. The former, a singer and elocutionist, presented many Shakespearean monologues and billed himself as "Shakespeare's Proud Representative."[23] Aldridge was born in 1807 and educated at the African Free School, located near the African Grove Theater. His interest in serious drama necessitated his living and working in Europe most of his life, for the most he could look forward to in America was working in blackface song and dance. In Europe he performed such roles as Othello, Macbeth, Shylock, and Lear.[24] Aldridge's success abroad demonstrates the existence of Black talent that found little outlet in the commercial theatres of America.

Black theatrical talent displayed itself in dramatic writing as well as in acting. There are four major Black dramatists of the nineteenth century whose plays are extant: Ira Aldridge and Victor Sejour, who both decided their work would best be received in Europe; and William Wells Brown and William Easton, who remained in the United States to use their writing in the struggle against slavery and racism. In 1893 Easton wrote: "Indeed we have had excellent caricatures of the Negro, in his only recognized school of legitimate drama, buffoonery."[25] Easton had an interest in serious drama, and he worked to provide scripts to counter caricatures of Blacks in theatre. He was credited with having written two militant verse plays, entitled *Dessalines* and *Christophe*.

William Wells Brown, a slave who ran away from Kentucky to Missouri and after reaching that free state was not allowed to remain free, made his way to Boston, educated himself, and began writing poetry, short stories, and novels. In 1856, he wrote his first play, entitled *Experience; or, How to Give a Northern Man a Backbone*, a farce about a White Boston minister who supported slavery but who during a visit to the South was accidentally sold into slavery, cruelly treated, and eventually freed. Brown's second play, *The Escape; or, A Leap for Freedom* became in 1858 the first play written by a Black to be published in the United States. The story treats a young Black slave couple who, after refusing to give up their dignity and virtue to the slave master, "leap for freedom" by leaving the country. Brown's drama was not performed on stage but instead read aloud at Abolitionist meetings.[26]

Black drama developed slowly in the century between Brown in 1859 and Lorraine Hansberry in 1959. However, Blacks during this time were in large measure responsible for America's major contribution to theatre history, the musical. Thomas Jefferson, a slaveowner and later President of the United States, testifies to the antiquity of Black musical entertainments in his *Notes on Virginia* (1784):

> In music they [the slaves] are generally more gifted than the whites, with accurate ears for tune and time, and they have been found capable of imagining a small catch [song]. The instrument proper to them is the banjar [banjo], which they brought hither from Africa.[27]

Aside from their obvious function as diversions for the slaves, these musical shows indirectly resisted oppression by obscurely ridiculing the slave masters; and many of the lyrics to the songs served as signals and messages to other slaves.

The first significant emergence of Black musical talent after the end of slavery was in the minstrel show. On June 5, 1881, the *New York Times* recounted how a White actor named Thomas "Daddy" Rice popularized "Ethiopian minstrelsy" and became known as "Jim Crow" Rice. Having watched Jim Crow, a physically deformed slave, dance a jig and fashion a song, Rice added verses to the song, exaggerated Crow's dance, and performed it in Louisville before an audience who so enjoyed the performance that they recalled him twenty times to repeat it.[28] "And so, Jim Crow," a caricature invented by Rice, "reinforcing the image of the black buffoon, jumped into the dramatic pantheon," according to *The Negro Almanac*.[29] Blacks often created songs and dances, and Whites exaggerated them, thereby inaugurating the age of the minstrel show.

The minstrels of these shows were White performers with burnt cork on their faces, outlined with white greasepaint. They formed a semicircular line-up to perform comic scenes, jigs, and other dances to popular songs about Negroes.[30] The minstrel show commonly featured five stereotypes of Blacks: the tragic mulatto, the buffoon, the Christian slave, the carefree primitive, and the black beast.[31] What had started out based in rudimentary realism thus developed into fantastic artificiality. *The Negro Almanac* reports that "White minstrels caricatured blacks and black music. . . . Blackface minstrel troupes gave their audiences music and dances 'borrowed' from blacks mixed with racist comedy routines."[32] The White takeover of minstrelsy succeeded in fixing deep in the subconscious of White Americans the idea that all Blacks were shiftless, lazy, thick-lipped watermelon eaters and gin guzzlers who abused the English language. Edith Isaacs credits the minstrelsy with "help[ing] to create and to fix the Negro stereotypes—passive or scheming, over-dull or over-shrewd, but always irresponsible and caricatured—which have burdened our theatre ever since, in American literature and in everyday life."[33] Nevertheless, Isaacs gives minstrelsy credit for being "our first authentic American theatre form. It left us the vaudeville monologue, many dance routines, the double forms of music that Isaac Goldberg calls 'music of the heels' and 'music of the heart.' And it trained many of the next generation of Negro singers, dancers, composers and comedians."[34]

Though the minstrel shows were unflattering to Blacks in many ways, they also provided a training ground in theatrical practices for many Blacks who entered theatre. After the Civil War, according to *The Negro Almanac*,

> Blacks formed their own groups. . . . These groups copied their white counterparts' style of blackened face with red and white outlines around the mouth. Audiences were segregated. . . . The important

thing . . . was that black people had finally achieved a tenuous access to the American stage.[35]

The most popular of the Black minstrels were the Georgia Minstrels organized in 1865 by Charles Hicks and featuring Billy Kersands and well-trained musicians. They toured England under the management of Jack Haverly in 1881 and were hailed as the greatest and largest minstrel show ever seen in England. After this tour, the Frohmans took over the management of the group and put them on a successful tour of the United States.[36]

Although minstrelsy continued after 1890, audiences' interest in it began to wane. "Americans had grown tired of minstrelsy," writes Haskins,

> and it seemed that they'd grown tired of seeing blacks on stage. The Abolitionist fervor had died away along with the commitment to black rights. As a part of this discouraging trend, white theatrical performers had become tired of sharing stages with blacks.[37]

Haskins means that Blacks were also performing minstrelsy on the stage, but they were still not allowed to perform in White companies or at the same time as White companies, and were allowed on those stages only when a White company was not available. However, Blacks interested in performing were determined to continue. Those who had performed in minstrel shows wanted to hone their skills and advance their fame.

With the turn of the century new faces emerged, but none more influential than Bert Williams and George Walker. Billing themselves as the "Two Real Coons," they were a successful team, Walker a fine comedian and Williams with a fine singing voice and skill with many musical instruments. Isaac states that

> Every trick of voice, inflection and gesture that Williams used was learned by careful study and observation. . . . [He] was the slouching, lazy, careless, unlucky Negro for whom everything went wrong. Walker was the dandy, the sporting Negro, dressed a little too high, spending generously whatever he was able to borrow or filch from

the Jonah Man's hard-earned money [and] from the very first night
the audience went wild about them.[38]

Also, around the turn of the century Blacks began writing musicals and
saw them produced on Broadway. In 1902, Williams and Walker
collaborated with playwright Will Marion Cook and director Jesse
Shipp and presented their first musical show, *In Dahomey*. A comic
show with original music, elaborate scenery, and a fully-fledged plot, it
played Broadway as the first successful Black musical. The show
incorporated African themes and characters, and yet the acting of
Williams and Walker was interesting and entertaining to White
American audiences. The piece was also performed in the Shaftsbury
Theatre located in London's Buckingham Palace. Performers who
traveled to London received first-class treatment but returned to face
prejudice in the United States. Black performers were sensitive to the
degree to which participation in "coon shows" may have demeaned
them. Bert Williams explained later in life how at eighteen he had
learned to temporize:

> I wouldn't do blackface. Nothing could have induced me to. So I
> worked straight and made $8 a week for a whole year. I awoke to the
> fact that $8 wasn't conducive to clean linen so I went to work using
> black cork. I got $50 a week then.[39]

In 1910 Williams was invited to join the Ziegfeld Follies, and since his
partner, George Walker, had become ill and retired from the stage,
Williams decided to accept the offer. A special role was written into the
show for him, but the rest of the cast refused to appear on the same
stage with him. After Abraham Erlanger, the company's producer,
worked out a compromise whereby Williams could perform on stage
alone, the applause Williams received was often so clamorous that the
next act had to wait to go on. After such success, the cast was glad to
work with him on stage, yet he was still segregated off stage. The other
performers did not want Williams to eat in the same restaurant or sleep
in the same hotel. He remained with the Ziegfeld Follies for ten years,
and from 1913 until 1917 he was the only Black artist working on
Broadway.[40]

Blacks were interested in performing serious plays, but much of the material available was either by Whites or was at least Eurocentric in style. Blacks with some experience constructing musicals began to write plays, and some of them won success. The first published play by a Black woman was *Rachel*, written by Angelina Grimke and produced by the National Association for the Advancement of Colored People (NAACP) in 1916. Grimke's father, a prominent journalist who served as United States Consul in Santo Domingo, served also for a time as vice-president of the NAACP. Therefore, Grimke was able to receive an education attainable by few Blacks or Whites at the time. Her play focused on racial discrimination, lynching, and a Black woman's refusal to bear any children in a world where prejudice would do them harm. *Rachel* became, according to Hatch, "the first Black play performed by Blacks, written by a Black to use the stage for race propaganda."[41]

One noticeable peculiarity of *Rachel* is that it was written without a trace of nonstandard idiom. That all Blacks spoke nonstandard English was a stereotype perpetuated by many White writers, and especially Ridgely Torrence[42] in the 'teens, Eugene O'Neill in the 'twenties, Marc Connelly in the 'thirties, and Tennessee Williams in the 'forties and 'fifties. Leslie Sanders explains that "Black audiences were uncomfortable with [White-written, non-standard] dialect [for Black characters] on stage because, traditionally, it provided much of the humor in the minstrel show and marked the black stage comic."[43]

The 1920s saw the emergence of more Black entertainers, more books by Blacks, and more Black university students. W. E. B. DuBois, for example, with a Ph.D. from Harvard in economics and history, was the founder and editor of *The Crisis Magazine*. DuBois deplored the fact that American Blacks had produced so little drama for Black audiences. Believing that the development of a real Black theatre was important to Blacks' self-image, he advanced four principles of Black drama. Black plays, he declared, ought to be

(1) About Us—Black drama must be about Blacks, with plots revealing Black life as it is; (2) By Us—the drama is written by Black authors who understand from birth and continual association what it means to be Black; (3) For Us—the drama caters to the Black

audience and is supported by them; and, (4) Near Us—the drama is performed in theatres located in Black neighborhoods.[44]

DuBois also wrote that

> If a man writes a play, and a good play, he is lucky if he earns first class postage upon it. Of course he may sell it commercially to some producer on Broadway; but in that case it would not be a Negro play or if it is a Negro play it will not be about the kind of Negro you and I know or want to know. If it is a Negro play that will interest us and depict our life, experience and humor, it can not be sold to the ordinary theatrical producer, but it can be produced in our churches and lodges, and halls.[45]

In 1925, Garland Anderson's *Appearances* became the first full-length drama by a Black playwright to reach Broadway. The play's three Black roles were portrayed by Black actors. This presented a problem, because according to Hatch, "Broadway policy in 1925 was to play 'colored' roles in blackface to avoid mixed casts."[46] However, David Belasco, the director, cast the roles with Blacks, whereupon two White cast members left the show. According to Hatch, again,

> Rehearsals had hardly begun [for *Appearances*] when a headline appeared "Nedda Harrigan Quits Play with Negro in the Cast." Miss Harrigan emphasized the fact that her decision must not be construed as indicative of race prejudice, but said that the production of a play called for so close an association with other players she felt that she could not be happy under the circumstances.[47]

In spite of this notoriety, the play went through a run of twenty-three performances in 1925 and was revived in 1929, when it ran for an additional twenty-four performances. *Appearances* was devoid of "Black" dialect, except for a small amount in the character of Rufus, an ignorant yet faithful servant. However, the lingering power of stereotypes caused the comic Rufus rather than the serious bellhop Carl to be considered the best role in the play. Likewise the theme of the play, though bold, had to come to terms with White expectations.

Anderson's conviction that, "As a man thinketh, so is he," was, according to Hatch,

> A brave one for 1925: a black man is falsely accused by a white woman. How did he dare present a white woman whose virtue was inferior to that of a black man? Mr. Anderson had to create a denouement for Broadway's satisfaction, and he did.[48]

Anderson wrote the character of Elsie Benton as a Black woman passing as White. The producers felt that this device permitted the character to be portrayed by a White rather than Black actress. Although this measure may have satisfied the commercial theatre and may have been necessary in order to get the play produced at all, it only dealt another blow to Black self-esteem and reinforced racial prejudice.

The Depression years resulted in a loss of jobs for over half of the American population, and actors were no exception. The Works Progress Administration (WPA), instituted by the Federal government, included a section called the Federal Theatre Project which employed actors and technicians. The Federal Theatre Project began in 1935 with Hallie Flanagan as its Director. Flanagan employed over 12,000 people in theatre units all over the country, including approximately 900 Blacks in segregated units. The New York Negro unit produced over fifty-five productions, one of the most famous of them being the "Voodoo *Macbeth*" directed by Orson Welles. Black productions, though mostly segregated, were able to balance their budgets and recover all the money spent on them during the life of the Federal Theatre Project. The Project ended in 1939, but not before many Whites had witnessed Black creativity and energy in the theatre.[49]

Individual Black playwrights and performers also received some recognition in the 1930s. In 1935 Langston Hughes' *Mulatto* opened on Broadway, ran for more than a year, and toured for two years. The play depicts an illicit interracial relationship in the South and a mulatto son's hatred of his White father. Rose McClendon, who had trained at the American Academy of Dramatic Arts, was the female lead. *Mulatto* set a record in its time for the number of performances of a play written by a Black, in spite of the fact that according to Mitchell, "Critics complained that the play was too realistic, too bitter and too hostile." [50]

The popular success of the play did not, however, translate into fame and fortune for its author. In fact, Hughes had difficulty collecting royalties and keeping control of his own play, for the director had other writers changing the script's text.

Paul Robeson was the first Black actor to achieve stardom by White standards, from the time of his first great successes in the 1920s. Robeson was approached by the Provincetown Players to perform the leads in Eugene O'Neill's *All God's Chillun' Got Wings* and a revival of *The Emperor Jones*. But despite achieving a certain amount of success, Robeson was shadowed by prejudice. According to Hatch, "In 1924, the press had demanded that the off-Broadway production of *All God's Chillun Got Wings* be banned because Paul Robeson kissed the hand of a white actress."[51] Despite such criticism, Robeson's success continued and he went to Europe, performing in *Emperor Jones* and *Othello*. In 1943, he played Othello at the Shubert Theatre in New York, giving 296 consecutive performances before packed audiences.

Robeson's renown, however, proved to be professionally fatal later when he publicly criticized the American government for its treatment of Blacks. Too influential a figure to be simply ignored, he was accused of trying to overthrow the government, a charge lent credibility by the post-war fear of Communism and its influence. Although Robeson was not convicted, he was forced to turn over his passport to the authorities and was forbidden to perform in this country or to travel and perform in any other country for eight years. In 1958, when his passport was returned, he moved to Europe and refused to accept the apologies of the United States.

The 1940s marked a decline of roles for Black actors in commercial theatre, and a general pattern of stereotypical roles and exploitation of Black characters continued. Hatch writes:

> White writers continued to exploit Negro characters in *Carmen Jones* (1943) and *Cabin in the Sky* (1940) Others substituted suffering Negroes for exotic Negroes in condescending plays like *Lost in the Stars* (1949), *The Respectful Prostitute* (1948), and *South Pacific* (1949). A few dramatists assayed the changes of attitude. *Deep Are the Roots* (1945) showed a black veteran returning home to the South,

but not to his "place." *Finian's Rainbow* (1946) used satire to tickle
the [racial] problem.[52]

Also in the 1940s, Dick Campbell and Frederick O'Neal began to
appeal to the Actors' Equity Association and the federal government
for laws to protect Blacks and Black culture from stage and film
presentations which degraded them. Although the actual laws which
would protect Blacks came later, these efforts fostered preliminary
legislation to halt the writing of prejudicial material about Blacks.
Furthermore, Actors' Equity was taking steps in the 1940s toward
desegregating American theatre.[53] This represented a breakthrough, for
Blacks at one time had been barred from this professional organization.
However, the Federal Theatre Project had been instrumental in
breaking the barriers to Black union membership. Once Blacks were
admitted in Actors' Equity, they registered complaints that the
organization had to address. The very recognition of Blacks by Actors'
Equity in the 1940s helped to discourage playwrights from writing
derogatory material about them. In the 1950s, Actors' Equity and other
theatrical unions drafted a statement which asserted that

> While caricature and stereotype are always to be condemned, there is
> nothing inherently wrong in comedy and servant roles when they are
> part of a living presentation. However, when Negro citizens are
> presented exclusively in such roles, an imbalance results, and their
> integration in American life is improperly set before the world. We
> must correct this situation, not by eliminating the Negro artist, but by
> enlarging his scope and participation in all types of roles and in all
> forms of American entertainment—just as in American life, the
> Negro Citizen's role now extends from the kitchen to the United
> Nations.[54]

Frederick O'Neal was elected president of Actors' Equity in 1964.
While serving for nine years, he was able to continue reforms for
Blacks in the Arts.

The American Negro Theatre Company [ANT], organized in 1940,
was one of many groups which had as its main thrust the
discouragement of segregation in the theatre.[55] It worked also, with the

cooperation of Actors' Equity, to deter negative representations of Blacks and Black life. The two principal founders were Abram Hill, a playwright, and Frederick O'Neal, an actor who had been associated with the Rose McClendon Players. Other members included Hilda Simms, Alice Childress, Alvin Childress, Earle Hyman, Canada Lee, Ossie Davis, Ruby Dee, and Frank Silvera. One of the company's concerns was to have no main star; it wanted to be viewed as a collective venture with no one person overshadowing another.

The ANT performed John Brown's *Natural Man* (1937), and Abram Hill's *On Striver's Row* (1940) and *Walk Hard* (1944), among others. But its biggest success came in 1944 with the play *Anna Lucasta*, written by Philip Yordan and adapted by Abram Hill. The play remained on Broadway for nearly three years, enjoyed 956 performances, and featured Frederick O'Neal, Canada Lee, Ossie Davis, Ruby Dee, Sidney Poitier, Frank Silvera, and John Proctor.[56] In the opinion of some Blacks, the play's success may not have been entirely deserved, for Mitchell writes that

> *Anna Lucasta,* for all its trailblazing, is a mediocre play. . . . It is a poor imitation of Eugene O'Neill's *Anna Christie,* which is not a very good play itself. And *Anna Lucasta* actually represents something vicious in terms of the double standard—namely, it suggests that the remedy for a bad play is to make it Negroid and it will succeed. And this time it worked. But the day that white audiences begin to see Negroes as people, this gimmick is going to be in trouble.[57]

The group felt that their play was good enough for Broadway's standards, and that became more important to them than the training workshops in acting that they had organized. More importantly, young actors wanted to join the group not for the aesthetic value of Black theatre but for conveyance to Broadway stardom. Ironically, "The very Star System its founders had sought to avoid destroyed its promise in the end."[58] Ethel Pitts Walker reports that "once the company lost sight of its initial objectives, set its sights on Broadway, and expanded its programs to a full-time school and a weekly radio series, the group began to decrease in excellence."[59] The group disbanded in the early 1950s.

In the 1950s the NAACP began to take legal action to end racism. The biggest triumph came in the verdict in the case of Brown v. The Board of Education of Topeka, Kansas, in which the United States Supreme Court declared segregation in the public schools of America unconstitutional. Mitchell, describing one such instance of segregation in Oklahoma, explains that

> In the case of McLaurin versus Oklahoma State Regents the law . . . in requiring that a Negro, admitted to a white graduate school, be treated like all other students, again resorted to tangible considerations . . . his ability to study, to engage in discussions, and exchange views with other students, and in general, to learn his profession. Such considerations apply with added force to children in grade and high schools. To separate them from others of similar age and qualifications solely because of their race generates a feeling of inferiority as to their status in the community that may affect their hearts and minds in a way unlikely to ever be undone. [60]

In 1957, Congress passed the first Civil Rights Act since 1875. This Act created a commission on Civil Rights, affirmed all citizens' right to vote, and demanded trial by jury rather than by judge for all civil rights cases.[61]

These legal victories evoked a reaction in the field of entertainment. Haskins offers the following explanation for this:

> As White playwrights and producers became more sensitive to racial discrimination, they realized that stereotyped stage roles like servants and comical characters were often racist. So they stopped including such roles in their plays. Unfortunately, they did not replace those roles with other parts for Blacks, and it seemed as if the Negro was in danger of being eliminated from the stage completely.[62]

During this period a creative and revolutionary spirit in Black theatre was afoot in off-Broadway theatres and in Greenwich Village. Dramatists such as Alice Childress, William Branch, and Loften Mitchell saw their works produced there, while, according to Haskins, the "Village as a whole was full of artistic energy."[63]

The greatest single breakthrough for American Black drama was the premiere of Lorraine Hansberry's *A Raisin in the Sun* (1959). Aside from its being the first play by a Black woman to appear on Broadway,[64] the play's text dispensed with stereotypes and showed Blacks as complex characters. It was also the first commercially successful Black play directed by a Black, Lloyd Richards. Woodie King, Jr., and Ron Milner write that *A Raisin in the Sun*

> marked a turning point, for until this time no black actor, black director, or technician had benefited financially from any of the plays about Black people that had been presented. It had always been a white producer or white writer who had profited.[65]

Audiences applauded *A Raisin in the Sun* and the performances of its cast, including Sidney Poitier, Ruby Dee, Claudia McNeill, Ivan Dixon, Lou Gossett, Jr., Ossie Davis, Glenn Turman, and Douglas Turner Ward. *A Raisin in the Sun* also won the New York Drama Critics' Circle Award for the Best Play of the 1958-1959 season, becoming the first Black play on Broadway to win a major award. At the age of twenty-nine, Hansberry became the first African-American and the youngest playwright ever to win the coveted award; she remains the only African-American woman ever to win it.

Although this breakthrough was monumental in many ways, it was not the step forward for Blacks that it appeared to be. According to Fabre, *A Raisin in the Sun* "ignores the values in the black world" and "embraces the supposedly universal white ideal."[66] Hansberry herself, in fact, asserted in an interview that her play was "not a black play, but a play about an American family in conflict with a corrupt society."[67] Yet the play's very universality, which is the key to its greatness as literature, diminishes its significance as a triumph in Blacks' struggle for respect on the Broadway stage. Not being uniquely Black, the play is not the ideal culmination to the efforts of the many playwrights, directors, actors, and critics who had striven for White acceptance for over a hundred years. Mitchell adds, in a note of irony, that

> *A Raisin in the Sun* crystallized the era Negro playwrights began to call the "nots." The critics said *In Splendid Error* [William Branch,

1954] was not a message play, *Trouble in Mind* [Alice Childress, 1955] was not vindictive, *Take a Giant Step* [Louis Peterson, 1953] was not just about Negroes, *Simply Heavenly* [Langston Hughes, 1957] was not an angry play, *A Land Beyond the River* [Loften Mitchell, 1957] was not a propaganda play, and *A Raisin in the Sun* was not a Negro play. In other words, Black playwrights were being praised for not making White people uncomfortable in the theatre.[68]

Commercial acceptance of Black plays had been a pursuit of Blacks since *The Chip Woman's Fortune*, Willis Richardson's, introduction to Broadway in 1923. Playwright and actor Ossie Davis wrote that for "too long had we Negro actors, playwrights, and directors fought to get onto Broadway and been, by and large, denied."[69] Only eleven Black playwrights had seen their plays produced on Broadway by 1959 and none until Hansberry had won an award.[70] It becomes evident that the commercial acceptance Blacks had worked so long to establish had become anticlimactic by 1959, coming as it did ahead of social acceptance.

Attitudes proved more resistant to change than box office sales or even the law. The Civil Rights Movement began in 1955, when Rosa Parks refused to move to the back of the bus. Her action began the Montgomery Boycott, which led to marches, sit-ins, riots, and chaos. Many Whites deplored the atrocities they witnessed on television, including attacks on Blacks by policemen employing dogs and water hoses. The 1950s ended with the brash declamations of Malcolm X, who advocated a violent "hate Whitey" dogma while Martin Luther King, Jr., advocated a non-violent, "love your enemy" doctrine.

In the 1950s, for most Blacks emancipation had meant assimilation into White culture. Africanisms, as mentioned earlier, had been a source of embarrassment in public, and accordingly Black drama had eschewed them as well. In the 1960s, however, the time had come for Blacks to reveal their true feelings. Many Blacks rejected or at least resisted Western traditions. Relaxed, straightened, processed hair and permanent waves were superseded by nappy hair and kinky Afros. Department store clothing gave way to dashikis and other forms of African dress. One might say, in fact, that the clothing and hairdos worn since the 1950s have served more to publicize Africanisms than to conceal them. Students called for Black History and emphasis on Black accomplishments to be taught in their schools and colleges. Black pride became an issue, Black History Month was revolutionized, and interest in the accomplishments of Blacks increased. Moreover, Black theatre increasingly rejected Western dramatic structure, form, and subject matter.

The Black Power Movement of the 1960s nurtured and fueled the Black Arts Movement. Paralleling the marches, sit-ins, and picketing were the revolutionary works of Amiri Baraka, Douglas Turner Ward, and Ron Milner. The explosions of physical violence were reflected in dramas such as Baraka's *The Dutchman* (1964), *The Toilet* (1964), and *The Slave* (1964), Ward's *Day of Absence* (1965) and *Happy Ending* (1965), and Milner's *Who's Got His Own* (1965). In the spring of 1968, Larry Neal wrote:

> The Black Arts and the Black Power concept both relate broadly to the Afro-American's desire for self-determination and nationhood. Both concepts are nationalistic. One is concerned with the relationship between art and politics, the other with the art of politics. Recently, these two movements have begun to merge: the political values inherent in the Black Power concept are now finding concrete expression in the aesthetics of Afro-American dramatists, poets, choreographers, musicians, and novelists.[71]

This declaration manifested itself in the dramas of Black playwrights who called for total independence of the white establishment: for a revolutionary theatre which attacked the racist systems of America; for a separatist theatre which was not interested in White participation or approval; and for a ritualistic theatre which disregarded traditional commercial concepts of success. Neal defined this Black Arts Movement as being radically opposed to an artist's alienation from his community and as "propos[ing] a radical reordering of the western cultural aesthetic" with "a separate symbolism, mythology, critique, and iconology." He argued that it was necessary "for Black people to define the world in their own terms, confront the contradictions arising out of the Black man's experience in the racist

West," and radicalize or destroy values inherent in Western history to make way for a "whole new system of ideas."[72]

One of the first playwrights to respond to this call for separation was Amiri Baraka, whose revolutionary theatre shocked America. According to Mitchell, the opening of *The Dutchman* in 1964 at the off-Broadway Cherry Lane Theatre "was auspicious. It was a fiery one-act play . . . charging that this is the pattern of America—seducing, tempting, insulting the black man, then killing him when he objects."[73] Baraka was bold with his descriptions of racism, and there seemed to be a parallel between his revolutionary theatre and that of DuBois, with the notable exception that Baraka managed to be abrasive enough that Whites could not ignore him. Hatch writes:

> In 1926, W. E. B. DuBois supervised the formation of the Krigwas, a theatre that was to produce plays *about* Negroes, *by* Negroes, *for* Negroes, and *near* Negroes. The white mass media did not exploit it, and white America remained unthreatened by a separatist art movement. In 1965, LeRoi Jones demanded a theatre *about* black people, *with* black people, *for* black people, and *only* black people. This time Caucasian fears arose righteously to denounce "reverse racism."[74]

Dutchman won the Obie Award, which hailed it as the best off-Broadway Play of the 1964-65 season. Yet Baraka did not follow up this spectacular success by capitalizing on the honor his award had brought him, nor did he ingratiate himself or his art with Whites. Quite the opposite. As Sanders puts it, "Having achieved phenomenal success on the mainstream stage, Baraka abandoned it and the criteria by which he had been so highly praised. His deliberate, dramatic gesture brought black theatre into a new phase."[75]

Baraka formed the Harlem Black Arts Repertory Theatre and School, which excluded Whites. At Baraka's theatre, according to Hatch, "White roles would be played in white face by black actors."[76] His plays were aimed at raising the consciousness of Blacks as an onslaught against racism, and for his efforts he was named by some "the angry playwright."[77] For his part Baraka continued his revolutionary ideas in plays such as *The Baptism* (1964), *Experimental*

Death Unit No. 1 (1964), *The Great Goodness of Life* (1965), and *Black Mass* (1965).

Hatch reports that "Since that day in 1965 when Imamu Baraka issued his manifesto, blacks in the theater have gradually educated blacks and whites to the values of a pluralistic society versus the losses in an assimilated one."[78] But the greater number of Black artists have stopped short of Baraka's contemptuous repudiation of White acceptance and aggressive exclusion of White participation. Ed Bullins, foremost member of this group, has been called "America's greatest playwright."[79] Williams writes that "Bullins' technique was to allow his characters to tell their own stories, revealing to each other and to the audience only what they want to." By employing this concept, "he never takes sides or imposes his own personal point of view upon the action."[80] Bullins himself said that he wanted a National Black Theatre which

> would be a medium for communication to raise the consciousness throughout the nation, for black artistic, political, and cultural consciousness. . . . [I]t would be an institution for the black people in America who are a nation within a nation. . . . It would be power in the sense of welding black artists and many disciplines, because the theater is a collective effort and many arts come together to get the spirit going. And we would get unity. . . . When you have a black theater and you have a black audience and a black artist—the idea of getting people back together is *passé*. The people *are* together and all you have to do while they are together is to tell them things which are beneficial and progressive.[81]

Bullins brought his plays and his ideology to the New Lafayette Theatre. These plays included *Clara's Ole Man* (1965), *Goin' a Buffalo* (1966), *In the Wine Time* (1968), *The Electronic Nigger* (1968), and *In New England Winter* (1971). Along with his plays Bullins wrote many Black rituals for the New Lafayette Theatre, and when this occurred the theatre began to lose its prominence. Bullins' rituals, although departures from Western traditional theatre, proved unsuccessful. They employed long titles and were slow and lethargic pieces of rhetoric which the audience could not understand or identify with. One such ritual, entitled *A Ritual to Bind Together and Strengthen Black People so that they can Survive the Long Struggle that is to Come*, had the audience sitting silently in the dark for a lengthy time. Williams makes it clear that the New Lafayette Theatre "was criticized for wasteful expenditures, for not using the best talent available, and for letting the artistic level of its productions drop considerably. For whatever reasons, NLT in the winter of 1972 voted itself out of existence."[82]

In 1965, Langston Hughes expressed sympathy for those motives that had fostered Bullins' attempt. He had, in fact, nurtured these same ideals since the beginning of his own career in the 1920s:

> There is a very great need for a serious theatre in the Harlem Community of New York City . . . a theatre in which the drama and the folk arts of the Negro people might be presented before the very audiences out of whom this drama is born. . . . Integration is wonderful, but culture must of necessity begin at home. I propose the creation of a National Afro-American Theatre.[83]

In this spirit of a new theatre for Blacks, then, Baraka advocated a theatre void of White participation; Ed Bullins asked for a National Black Theatre; and Langston Hughes asked for a theatre in Harlem for Blacks, urging that it be named The National Afro-American Theatre. This spirit argued for a theatre separate from White theatre in location, ideology, and dramatic structure, a theatre dedicated to educating, informing, and entertaining Blacks. Baraka, Bullins, and Hughes agreed that theatre needed to raise the consciousness of Blacks, to be politically active, and to move toward establishing greater unity within the Black race. At the end of the 1960s, there arose a Black theatre which tried to accomplish all these goals—and it was a Black woman, a member of one of the most oppressed groups in America, who founded this theatre.

Into this politically conscious New York theatre scene came Barbara Ann Teer. In 1968 she expressed her own belief in the futility of the assimilationist route to success and in the need for separation in Black theatre:

Up to now, the Negro artist has been totally concerned with
integration, with finding a place for his creative talents in the existing
theatre. He has spent thousands of dollars on classes and training, and
countless years of frustration, to compete in an already established,
highly competitive industry. Clearly he feels that if he can just make
it to Broadway, he will have reached the pinnacle of success. . . . In
the process of trying to realize this dream, he has had to picket, sit-in,
march, and even in various theatrical unions, negotiate new rules to
provide more employment. The situation for the Negro in the theatre
and other mass media remains frighteningly depressing. How long
will it take him to . . . realize . . . how he is being used—or how he
has allowed himself to be used—by the white establishment? . . . I
believe the need for a Black art form is far more critical even than the
issue of white racism. And the Negro artist must examine the need
for a Black cultural art form before he can take any step forward.[84]

Larry Neal reports that "After *Dutchman* . . . a multitude of other
theaters [sprang from] its basic model: a theater in the community, and
a manifesto for the theater as a total nationalist institution, a reflection
in miniature of the entire nation, which was meant above all to be an
instrument for the raising of political, ethical, and aesthetic
consciousness."[85] Teer, a contemporary of Neal and Baraka, was in the
process of organizing a theatre much in keeping with Neal's views and
with Baraka's manifesto. She believed that the formation of the
National Black Theatre was an effort to counteract the damage done to
Black people in America by centuries of prejudice, racial
discrimination, and myths about Blacks, believed not by Whites alone
but by Blacks themselves. The long history of oppression had made the
ill-feeling that Whites felt for Blacks, and the shame and contempt that
Blacks felt for themselves, seem like a normal state of affairs to
oppressor and oppressed alike. Before the 1960s, the theatre had often
done little more than reflect, and hence reinforce, the societal
oppression which Teer wanted to remedy. What Black people—and
children especially—saw and heard, they often believed, and the
images of Blacks that stage, film, radio, and television offered them
were usually stereotypes: the mammy, the simpleton, the savage, and
the Christian servant. Actors such as Stepin Fetchit, Hattie McDaniels,

Butterfly McQueen, and radio characters such as Beulah and Amos 'n' Andy were just a few of the Blacks seen and heard in stereotypical roles. The Tarzan films provided the ultimate degradation, showing Blacks not only as servants but as savages and cannibals. Hatch writes:

> The American motion picture industry since its inception has perpetuated the idea of the superiority of white Anglo-Saxons. All other races have been subjected to ridicule, caricature, mockery. . . . but the black stereotype has remained the longest. [86]

Plays such as Eugene O'Neill's *Emperor Jones* (1920), Dorothy and DuBose Heyward's *Porgy* (1927), Marc Connelly's *Green Pastures* (1930), and Tennessee Williams' *Cat on a Hot Tin Roof* (1955) helped to reinforce the lesson that Blacks were naturally inferior to White people—uneducated, and happy to be good servants.

The 1960s were turbulent years, and 1968 was no exception. The conviction and sentencing of Amiri Baraka in January, the April assassination of Martin Luther King, Jr., and the riots which followed were succeeded by the Poor People's March on Washington in May and the assassination of Robert Kennedy in June, 1968—events that daunted and dismayed Blacks and Whites alike. Blacks had lost the greatest civil rights leaders they had ever known. How could the healing begin? Who would lead them to fight against injustice? What future lay ahead for them as many hung their heads in resignation? Blacks were looking to feel strong again. Many turned to theatre.

Teer cried out to her students in one class session, "Don't use your energy to hate the white man, use your creative energy to better yourself."[87] And looking back in 1980 she declared,

> Our [NBT's] standard of art was designed to present black people in a way that supported and strengthened and nurtured who they were, because as a subculture in a dominant culture, we were not included. We inherited a legacy of "less-than-ness." . . . My processes were designed to give people a sense of wholeness, a sense of rightness with themselves. Once that was done, there was no longer a need for separation.[88]

To cure the less-than-ness feelings in Blacks, Teer offered a theatrical ideology and training. Her goal was to help correct feelings of inferiority not only for performers but also for every audience that came to see them. Although Teer was not familiar with the history of Black theatre or Western traditional theatre, she was very familiar with Black history and the pain of living in a society characterized by cultural hegemony. It was this pain that she sought to alleviate through the formation of the National Black Theatre.

NOTES

1. Bruce McConachie, "Using the Concept of Cultural Hegemony to Write Theatre History," *Interpreting the Theatrical Past: Essays in Historiography of Performance*, eds. Thomas Postlewait and Bruce McConachie (Iowa City: University of Iowa Press, 1989), p. 46.

2. Ironically (if the recent scholarship of Martin Bernal is valid) Greek culture itself may have Afro-Asiatic roots, a fact gradually but systematically expunged from history during the nineteenth century. See Martin Bernal, *Black Athena: The Fabrications of Ancient Greece, 1785-1935* (New Brunswick, N.J.: Rutgers University Press, 1987), p. 163.

3. James V. Hatch, "Here Comes Everybody: Scholarship and Black Theatre History," *Interpreting the Theatrical Past*, p. 150.

4. Formerly known as LeRoi Jones, he changed his name during the 1960s to Imamu Amiri Baraka. In recent years he has eliminated the name Imamu ("Spiritual Leader") in keeping with his Marxist views, which discourage leadership. In this dissertation he will be referred to as Amiri Baraka, except when those quoted employ his former name.

5. Amiri Baraka, *Blues People: Negro Music in White America* (New York: William Morrow & Co., 1963), p. 12.

6. Baraka, p. 13. Additionally, Mance Williams reports that "African oral tradition formulated and passed down the concepts of existence and essence through poems, songs, music, and oral history" (*Black Theatre in the 1960s and 1970s: A Historical-Critical Analysis of the Movement* [Westport, Connecticut: Greenwood Press, 1985], pp. 33-34).

7. Hatch, p. 155.

8. Baraka, p. 13.

9. Genevieve Fabre, *Drumbeats, Masks, and Metaphor* (Cambridge, Massachusetts: Harvard University Press, 1983), p. 219.

10. Linda James Myers, "The Nature of Pluralism and the African American Case," *Theory into Practice*, 20 (1981), 5.

11. Hatch, p. 155.

12. "We Wear the Mask": We wear the mask that grins and lies, / It hides our cheeks and shades our eyes,—/ This debt we pay to human guile; / With torn and bleeding hearts we smile, / And mouth with myriad subtleties. / Why should the world be overwise, / In counting all our tears and sighs? / Nay, let them only see us, while / We wear the mask. / We smile, but, O great Christ, our cries / To Thee from tortured souls arise. / We sing, but oh, the clay is vile / Beneath our feet, and long the mile; / But let the world dream otherwise, / We wear the Mask." In *Black Voices: An Anthology of Afro-American Literature* (New York: New American Library, 1968), p. 355.

13. James A. Anderson, "Cognitive Styles and Multicultural Populations," *Journal of Teacher Education*, January-February 1988, 5.

14. "The Constitution of the United States," *Afro USA*, ed. Harry Ploski and Ernest Kaiser (New York: Bellwether Publishing Company, Inc., 1971), p. 100.

15. "The Black Entertainer in the Performing Arts," *The Negro Almanac,* ed. Harry Ploski and James Williams (New York: John Wiley and Sons, 1983), p. 807.

16. Serious research on the development of its history began slowly in the 20th century from newspapers, articles, and the collection of books, papers, and articles, particularly at the Schomburg Library on African American History.

17. *The Negro Almanac*, p. 805.

18. Edith Isaacs, *The Negro in the American Theatre* (New York: Theatre Arts, Inc., 1947), p. 13.

19. James Haskins, *Black Theater in America* (New York: Thomas Y. Crowell, 1982), p. 6. Unfortunately, the play is not extant.

20. Loften Mitchell, *Black Drama: The Story of the American Negro in the Theatre* (New York: Hawthorn Books, Inc., 1967), p. 25.

21. Haskins, p. 9.

22. Haskins, p. 9.

23. Haskins, p. 6.

24. Haskins, pp. 6, 9-14.

25. Hatch, *Black Theatre U.S.A.* (New York: The Free Press, 1974), p. 2.

26. Haskins, p. 17. "Brown's play . . . written one year after the Dred Scott Decision and one year before John Brown's raid, criticized corruption in the South, but it catered to the melodramatic tastes of the day. William Wells Brown fought for emancipation, and his voice carried some weight. But he never managed to champion the cause of black playwrights in American theatre." In Fabre, p. 250.

27. *The Negro Almanac,* p. 808.

28. *The New York Times*, Sunday, June 5, 1881, triple sheet, col. 3.

29. *The Negro Almanac*, p. 808

30. *The Negro Almanac*, p. 809.

31. Haskins, pp. 25-27.

32. *The Negro Almanac*, pp. 808-09.

33. Isaacs, p. 27.

34. Isaacs, p. 27.

35. *The Negro Almanac*, p. 809.

36. Haskins, p. 28.

37. Haskins, p. 31.

38. Isaacs, p. 35.

39. Quoted in Hatch, *Black Theatre U.S.A.*, p. 618.

40. Haskins, pp. 43-44.

41. Hatch, *Black Theatre U.S.A.*, p. 137.

42. Ridgely Torrence, a White poet, wrote three one-act plays containing 'music conducted and performed by Blacks." The plays—*Granny Maumee, The Rider of Dreams*, and *Simon the Cyrenian*, known as *Three Plays for a Negro Theatre*—opened at the Old Garden Theatre on April 5, 1917. Mitchell reports that "Torrence's dramas must have played better than they read . . . Torrence's written text is embarrassingly clumsy, his Negro speech earthbound, and his themes seem remote from the actual experience of black people on this continent. While Torrence may have assisted in paving the way for the Negro to reenter the downtown theatre, he also assisted in fathering a long line of neo-stereotype characters that ranged from the Emperor Jones to Abraham to Porgy to those of the present" (69). Mitchell's criticism of Torrence's plays by Hatch, who notes that Torrence's "dialect transcription . . . approaches cryptography:—Oh, whuffo dee drag me out an' hilt me back? I bo'one man an' him dee tuk 'n bu'nt. An' 'e slep' right 'n dis room w'en de man wuz shot w'ich dee 'cuze 'im er!" Though Torrence's plays continued to perpetuate the stereotype that Blacks could speak only in a hard-to-understand dialect, their

performances marked one of the first times anywhere in the United Stated that Black actors in the dramatic theatre "commanded the serious attention of the critics and the general public." p. 178.

43. Leslie Sanders, *The Development of Black Theatre: From Shadows to Selves* (Baton Rouge: Louisiana State University Press, 1988), p. 32.

44. W. E. B. DuBois, "The Little Theatre of the Krigwa Players," *Crisis Magazine*, vol. 32, no. 3, (July, 1926), 134.

45. W. E. B. DuBois, "The Negro Art," *Crisis Magazine*, vol. 32, no. 6, (Oct., 1926), 290.

46. Hatch, *Black Theatre U.S.A.*, p. 100.

47. Hatch, *Black Theatre U.S.A.*, p. 100.

48. Hatch, *Black Theatre U.S.A.*, p. 101.

49. Isaacs, pp. 86-97.

50. Mitchell, p. 97.

51. Hatch, *Black Theatre U.S.A.*, p. 392.

52. Hatch, *Black Theatre U.S.A.*, p. 391.

53. Haskins, p. 128.

54. Haskins, p. 131.

55. Haskins, p. 115.

56. Haskins, pp. 115-18.

57. Mitchell, pp. 122-23.

58. Haskins, pp. 117-18.

59. Ethel Pitts Walker, "The American Negro Theatre," *The Theatre of Black Americans*, ed. Errol Hill (New York: Applause Theatre Book Publishers, 1987), 259.

60. Mitchell, p. 172.

61. Lerone Bennett, Jr., *Before the Mayflower, A History of Black America*, 5th ed. (Chicago: Johnson Publishing Company, Inc., 1982), p. 554.

62. Haskins, p. 130.

63. Haskins, p. 131.

64. Hatch writes, "No play by a black woman had been produced on or off-Broadway before 1952, when Alice Childress' *Gold through the Trees* was presented off-Broadway" (In *Black Theatre U.S.A.*, p. 711). Bernard L. Peterson, Jr., writes that Alice Childress' *Trouble in Mind* was "First produced off-Broadway, at the Greenwich Mews Theatre, opening November 4, 1955, for 91 performances." It "received the Obie Award in 1956 as the best original off-Broadway play of the season. It marked the first major award received by a

female for playwriting. Although scheduled for a Broadway production in April 1957, under the title *So Early Monday Morning*, it was withdrawn by the author because of changes which the director wished to make" (In *Contemporary Black American Playwrights and Their Plays: A Biographical Directory and Dramatic Index* [New York: Greenwood Press, 1988], p. 107).

65. Woodie King, Jr., and Ron Milner, eds. *Black Drama Anthology* (New York: New American Library, 1971), p. vii.

66. Fabre, p. 3.

67. *New York Times*, October 11, 1964, sec. 2, 3.

68. Mitchell, p. 182.

69. Ossie Davis, "The Flight from Broadway," *Negro Digest* 15 (April 1966),16.

70. Mance Williams, p. 80.

71. Larry Neal, "The Black Arts Movement," *The Drama Review* 12 (Summer 1968), 29.

72. Neal, 29.

73. Mitchell, p. 199.

74. Hatch, *Black Theatre U.S.A.*, p. 773.

75. Sanders, p. 174.

76. Hatch, *Black theatre U.S.A.*, p. 812.

77. Mitchell, p. 127.

78. Hatch, p.774.

79. Marvin X, "An interview with Ed Bullins: Black Theatre," *Negro Digest* 18 (April 1969),14.

80. Williams, p. 24.

81. Marvin X, 12-13.

82. Williams, pp. 56-57.

83. Langston Hughes, "The Need For An Afro-American Theatre," in *The International Library of Negro Life and History-Anthology of the American Negro in The Theatre*, 2nd ed. ed. Lindsay Patterson (New York: Publishers Company, Inc., 1969), 163.

84. Barbara Ann Teer, "The Great White Way is Not Our Way—Not Yet," *Negro Digest* 17 (April 1968), 24, 25, 28.

85. Larry Neal, "Into Nationalism, Out of Parochialism," In *The Theatre of Black Americans*, 296.

86. Hatch, *Black Theatre U.S.A.*, p. 655.

87. Barbara Ann Teer, Identity, Dignity, and Trust Class, Saturday, October 24, 1987, at the National Black Theatre Classroom.

88. Gary Schoichet, "Barbara Ann Teer," *Other Stages*, April 17, 1980, 2.

II
Barbara Ann Teer: Background

There ain't nothing can happen to me
If it doesn't first happen thru me
So nothing can happen to me
Unless it passes thru my mind
You're the only one who can make yourself happy
You're the only one who can fill your life with joy
You're the only one who can make yourself happy
'Cause nothing can happen to you
Unless it passes thru your mind.

Barbara Ann Teer, *Soljourney into Truth*, 1979

Barbara Ann Teer has always believed in the autogenesis of dignity, confidence, and esteem. In the 1960s many Blacks blamed Whites for their circumstance in life. Teer felt that this negativity would defeat Blacks, increasing their hopelessness and pain. Pain, she believed, could be salutary but only if it instigated treatment of an underlying problem. Teer wrote in 1984:

All that is present, is a conversation we are having among ourselves, talking about the injustices of slavery, oppression, suffering, poverty and pain. And I assert that this conversation has limited our future possibilities here in America.[1]

In this same article she wrote that what was needed was a "new enthusiasm [generated] to give us the guts to keep re-defining, re-educating and restructuring our lives."[2] To this end, Teer advocated a theatrical theory which would combine African, or more specifically Yoruba traditions, and the ecstatic elements of the Black Pentecostal church of America. The combination of these two forces would nourish in many Blacks a spirit of freedom similar to that sustained in many Black slaves by religion. As Clifton Brown has explained,

> The foundation of Black religion in America, conceived as it was against a background of slavery and segregation, provided the Black man with the opportunity to be free while still in chains. Black religion produced a gospel of future hope.[3]

What Teer offered was a new conversation, a new way of thinking and being, a new paradigm arising from a discourse of self empowerment and self determination. Her theatre would reinforce the African tradition of collective and communal spirit which she called God Conscious Art. Teer defined God Conscious Art as one which produces an overwhelming creative force and energy that spontaneously swells from within. Its purpose is to build entrepreneurial artists to provide community-based positive leadership.

This chapter focuses on Teer's biography and the founding of the National Black Theatre, a theatre which combined western and African theatrical traditions of materialism and spirituality rooted in west African Yoruba cultural traditions and emerging in the new western world as a tradition with practices found in the Black Pentecostal church. The traditions of Yoruba Africans and certain forms of worship in the Black Pentecostal church will be explored and related to Teer's theatrical theory. Teer's ideology will be examined in its counteraction of the ill-effects of cultural hegemony.

Teer is the founder, spiritual leader, and prime mover of The National Black Theatre of Harlem. She is listed in *Who's Who* as an "actress, playwright, producer, educator, author, dancer, entertainer, musician, and real estate broker."[4] Teer was born on June 18, 1937, in East St. Louis, Illinois, the daughter of parents who "were very involved with improving the quality of life for Black people."[5] Her father, Fred Teer, now deceased, was a high school civics teacher and track coach. During his life he owned a newspaper, a printing shop, and two restaurants, and he served as assistant mayor of East St. Louis. Teer's mother, Lila, also a teacher, community developer, and activist is now retired. Both Teer's parents were well known in East St. Louis, and Teer was nurtured in a positive environment, growing "up proud and precocious," as she says of herself.[6]

The young Barbara and her sister Fredrica (1936-1979), learned dancing at their aunt's private dance school in East St. Louis. Teer was an accomplished student, her goal being "to dance her way to bright lights in a big city."[7] Thus, in college she decided to major in dance education. Teer, who describes herself as "overeducated,"[8] attended four American universities, starting at Bennett College in Greensboro, North Carolina, and continuing at the University of Illinois, Connecticut College, and then the University of Wisconsin. She was finally graduated with high honors after returning to the University of Illinois, receiving a Bachelor of Arts Degree in dance education in 1957 at the age of nineteen.[9] When asked why she attended so many universities, Teer replied that she had been taught by her parents that when you study under the "masters" you become inspired to be one yourself. If she read a book or magazine about a promising teacher who was teaching at another university, she transferred to that institution. She transferred to the University of Illinois, for example, when she learned that Mary Wigman, the pioneer of modern dance in Berlin had sent one of her associates, Margaret Dietz, to America to teach the Wigman techniques as a visiting professor there.[10]

After graduation, Teer went to Europe with Dietz as her protégé to study with Mary Wigman in Germany at the Wigman School of Dance. While in Europe she also studied pantomime with Etienne Decroux in Paris and performed in dance festivals throughout Switzerland. Returning to the United States, Teer studied with choreographer Alwin Nikolais at the Henry Street Playhouse. He was a Wigman, Honya Holm derivative, who taught dance as an abstract expression using electronic sound to characterize his creative visions. She joined the Alvin Ailey Dance Company and performed with them in Brazil.

She launched her Broadway career as the dance captain in *Kwamina*, choreographed by Agnes DeMille in 1961. However, a knee injury "forced [her] to set aside her dancing career."[11] Depressed by her injury, Teer consulted a spiritualist who told her that her power was in her voice rather than in her feet. It was then that she turned to acting, supporting herself by teaching dance at Wadleigh Junior High School in Harlem while studying acting with Sanford Meisner, Paul Mann, Philip Burton, and Lloyd Richards, among others.[12] "Acting," she says, "gave me discipline; it gave me an ability to expand my mental power because I could begin to look into, to analyze, to prove why people do things; [and understand] what are people's attitudes."[13]

In 1965, Teer won the Vernon Rice Drama Desk Award for her performance in Rosalyn Drexler's *Home Movies* (1964) and was in the original casts of Douglas Turner Ward's *Day of Absence* (1966) and Ron Milner's *Who's Got His Own* (1966). She also appeared in films including *Gone Are the Days* (1964), the film version of Ossie Davis' *Purlie Victorious* (1961), and *The Pawnbroker* (1965). Teer was known not only in the theatre and film worlds but in television as well, from her appearances on *The Ed Sullivan Show*, *Camera Three*, *Kaleidoscope*, and other programs. She also performed with Pearl Bailey in Las Vegas and with Duke Ellington in Chicago.[14]

Teer began writing for several periodicals and newspapers, including the *Black Theatre Magazine*, *Black Power Revolt*, *Black World*, and the *New York Times*. And yet with all these accomplishments, she was not content. In 1968 she wrote:

> As a Black actress, I can merely look forward to playing "demanding" roles such as prostitutes, maids, some form of the exotic, a role in one of the classics, and when I'm old and gray, I can look forward to playing a strong, forceful, ball-cutting matriarch. It's really amazing to what lengths playwrights and directors go to in order to make their Black characters fit the stereotype. . . . I had all this technique, all this ability; and I could not force it into these little narrow, one-dimensional parts. . . . So I found that I was a very unhappy person.[15]

Teer was unhappy not only with the roles she obtained but with the climate of the commercial theatre. She was becoming aware of who she was—a Black woman in the 1960s—and she stated, "So there I was politically aware, but in white theatre."[16] She was unhappy with the discrimination and double standard of commercial theatre and with "the limitations of being a woman and being black."[17] In an interview with Valerie Harris, Teer stated:

> I was an actress in my own right, what they call, "young actress on the rise," and in the middle of being that I just got sick of the whole thing, sick of being "less than," of experiencing my power, of having someone telling me to do something that didn't make sense to me. So I left.[18]

Teer not only left Broadway; she left New York in 1967.

Three specific incidents caused her to re-evaluate her goals: First, after becoming politically aware, she had her hair done in the popular style of the era, a "natural" or "Afro." Her White manager was furious yet sent her to an audition to read for a role. The director looked at her briefly and asked her to remove her hat. When she informed him that it was not a hat but her hair, he allowed her to read for the part, told her she gave a beautiful reading, and said that he would call her. But he did not call. When her manager insisted that she change her hairstyle, she refused.

Second, she was in rehearsal for an off-Broadway production when the director asked her to roll her eyes like Butterfly McQueen in the film *Gone with the Wind*. To Teer his remark was demeaning and insulting. Offended by the director's insensitivity in this and other areas, she eventually left the show.

Third, she was in another production with an all-Black cast, whose directors, producers, and technicians were all White. When Teer began to question the absence of Black technicians, she was labeled a trouble-maker and asked to leave the show. Teer stated, "I made a lot of people uncomfortable. People would say, 'you're militant,' or 'you're a professional black woman.'"[19] Most of her show business friends, Black and White, began to drift away, disturbed by Teer's new attitude. More disappointed than hurt, Teer said, "I began to realize that this whole system is corrupt, the image it creates is completely decadent. There is no such thing as art as I think of it."[20] Rather than embrace the "corruption" longer, Teer fired her manager, fired her agent, and returned home to East St. Louis.

East St. Louis is a predominantly Black community which fosters interest in the arts. Each elementary student is required to take lessons in playing a musical instrument and is encouraged to have training in singing, dancing, acting, and the visual arts. The town boasts such offspring as Miles Davis; Ike and Tina Turner; the poets Sherman Fowler, Eugene Redmond, and Henry Dumas; President Carter's United Nations Ambassador, Donald McHenry; Olympic Gold Medalist Jackie Joyner; comedian Dick Gregory; performer Josephine Baker; and the Black Sports Activist Harry Edwards. Kathryn Dunham, a Black dancer who popularized Caribbean and African Dance in America, selected East St. Louis as the headquarters for her dance school, which teaches Dunham's original dances.

Teer remained in East St. Louis for four months. Her return to New York was induced by an invitation to direct a show at the Public School Ninety-Two Theatre in Harlem as a benefit for Amiri Baraka, who had been jailed. She named the production, "We Sing a New Song." Her New York directing debut came with the off-Broadway production of *The Believers*, which was an artistic and financial success. She resumed working, along with Robert Hooks, as acting coach for the students of the Group Theatre Workshop creating a musical production from the Gwendolyn Brooks' eight-line Pulitzer-prize winning poem, *We Real Cool*. It was produced by Joseph Papp and traveled as a mobile unit all over New York.

Teer enjoyed this new-found creative outlet, working with Blacks on Black shows in a Black community, and she felt artistically fulfilled. Many of the cast members from *The Believers* wanted to study privately with Teer. However, Teer continued working with Robert Hooks and the students of the Group Theatre Workshop who were also involved with the productions of Douglas Turner Ward's *Day of Absence* and *Happy Ending*.

The Group Theatre Workshop evolved into the Negro Ensemble Company in the summer of 1967, but Teer decided to leave because, as she stated, "My philosophy was that we should not be called Negroes. And we should not be located in Greenwich Village. I didn't want to prove to white people that I could do their western art form as good as they could."[21] Teer and her followers left the group, they moved to Harlem and they began to distinguish themselves from Ward and other contemporaries. Teer was adamant in her determination not to perform contemporary or Black theatre based in a Western tradition. She wanted a theatre in tune with the spirit of W. E. B. DuBois and his Krigwa Players of Harlem in the 1920s, who felt that Black theatre should be about Black people, for Black people, near Black people, and by Black people. Teer stated:

> It therefore seems at this point our best and most realistic hope is to go back home, back to the Black community, and begin to build a "new theatre." A theatre that is not Broadway-oriented, a theatre where you can "call the shots" as you see them, and not be afraid of losing your job. A theatre where you will be free to experiment and to create. A theatre where you can relax and be "colored." ("Colored" in speech, movement, and behavior patterns.) A theatre where you can stop denying and begin identifying. Then, and only then, will you be able to create a power base which will allow you to become self-assertive.[22]

She felt concerned that Black theatre was merely an imitation of Western traditional theatre and American theatre, and with only limited participation by Blacks. "We are a race of people with a dual cultural heritage," Teer stated, and added that

> In the field of jazz and rhythm-and-blues, our identity is clearly reflected. We are American with an African ancestry! What an exciting theatrical combination! We should not have to choose which one of these combinations we wish to project. One enhances the other. It's like meat and potatoes, bread and butter, greens and cornbread. One makes the other taste better.[23]

Teer felt that Black performers "should begin to create artistically and realistically the strength, force, sense, and soul of Black people."[24] It was important to her that her theatre show how Black people are and how they could be. In addition, it was also important to have a theatre that could educate Whites concerning the feelings of Blacks. Ruby Dee, an established Black actress, argued along similar lines in her article, "The Tattered Queens":

> The reality is that we are but 10 per cent of a population which is geared to segregate and to discriminate—improving, I believe, but desperately in need of artistic effort to help change the image of the Negro and so effect social change more quickly. As art not only reflects life but also influences it, we must dedicate ourselves to the improvement of life and its truths about Negroes.[25]

Teer wanted a theatre that would promote esteem for Blacks and their accomplishments. In an interview with the *New York Post*, Teer claimed that at her theatre she was actually "rehabilitating black people's ability to love themselves"; furthermore, she stated, "If you don't have an experience of self-worth and are not in touch with who you are, you can't move through the world with any certainty."[26] She wanted to see an end to plays about Blacks written or directed by Whites who did not understand the Black experience. And she wanted to attend a theatre where she could see a play which validated her as a Black woman and could leave feeling exhilarated.

Teer sought to transcend prevailing forms of theatre. Within the prescribed formulas of Western traditional theatre, there are generally directors and actors, a theatre space, and a script—but each of these with limitations. The playwright limits, through the script, what can or will be said, and the director defines the style and can restrict movement. There can be audience interaction, but only at the discretion of the director. Teer stated that in traditional theatre,

> You're not free to be spontaneous and to let go because the form is more important than the feeling. . . . What the other Black theatres are doing is fine, within that form, but I wanted to add to the form, transform the form, actually, open it up so that we could really express our magnitude, our omnipotence, our fire.[27]

Teer's commitment to openness of form was elaborated by her enumeration of What-ifs: What if more emotion was needed than was specified by the playwright or director? What if more gesturing was

needed than was allowed by the director? What if the actor saw the
audience being moved and wanted to reach out further to them? Teer
saw any restriction as a handicap to the emotive force of the performer.
In establishing her theatre she was unyielding on three points:

(1) She did not want to be located in the commercialized
Greenwich Village;

(2) She did not want to do European plays or American traditional
standard plays but instead wanted large-scale shows with music and
spectacle;

(3) She was not interested in doing any type of theatre that Whites
were doing.[28]

Teer's move from Broadway to Harlem led to the formation of The
National Black Theatre. She explained that while other theatres were
building their philosophy of "what is," she herself built the NBT on the
philosophy of "what might be," "what is possible," "what's missing,"
and "what can we provide for what's missing."[29] Teer also wished to
establish a theatre that would promote performers' pride in their
performance, their accomplishments as artists, and their
accomplishments as Black persons. Blacks, she believed, needed also
to begin to recognize Africa as the "mother country." Teer felt that
Blacks needed to think positively of the wealth of the motherland and
of its rich cultural and artistic heritage. She wrote that "The Black actor
is the beneficiary of a rich cultural heritage, and the day has got to
come when he will be allowed to expose this image on every stage in
the American Theatre!"[30]

These, then, were the convictions that spurred Teer to begin her
own theatre. Teer knew that a theatre would encompass more than
actors. She needed plays. When asked by Valerie Harris to define Black
drama, Teer replied:

> I don't define it. I don't know what "Black drama" is. I just know that
> I'm a certain way, and that way nurtures me, and that's all I know to
> write about. . . . See, I don't separate dance from singing from writing
> from directing. There's really only the experience.[31]

Although Teer knew of no plays or scripts which expressed this
nurturing feeling she missed, she felt that what she wanted was an

artistic form which highlighted the positive aspects of Blacks, containing music, songs, and dances which would combine the African roots of Blacks with Christian inspiration.

Teer's search for experiences which would nurture her artistic expression led her to the Pentecostal church, whose spiritual exercises exactly suited her needs. According to Jessica Harris, Teer's process of creating a new Black actor is a spiritual experience:

> Most black people in the world are united by a common tradition of worship that cuts across social classes and national differences. This is not a common religion but rather a similarity of worship that can be traced through the religions of Africa to those of the Caribbean and finally to the Pentecostal and "holy roller" churches in the United States. It is from this energy that the NBT works to create a liberator.[32]

Three areas need to be examined next in order to understand the phenomenon of the "holy roller" church: (1) what is meant by a "Pentecostal" church; (2) how a typical Pentecostal service is conducted; and (3) the essential Blackness of Pentecostal worship, as evidenced by its relationship to modern-day Yoruba traditions.

BLACK PENTECOSTALISM

According to George Eaton Simpson, the Black Pentecostal movement originated at a 1906 revival conducted in Los Angeles, California,[33] by Reverend William J. Seymour, "a direct descendant of third generation African slaves."[34] Simpson further claims that "Pentecostalism expanded rapidly and by 1972 there were approximately two hundred Pentecostal denominations in the United States."[35] These denominators are characterized, according to Malcolm Calley, as Fundamentalists and Millenialists believing in baptism by total immersion and the "baptism of the Spirit evidenced by talking in tongues."[36] The Pentecostals use the King James Version of the Bible, believing literally in Acts 2: 1-4, which states:

1) And when the day of Pentecost was fully come, they were all with one accord in one place. 2) And suddenly there came a sound from heaven as of a rushing mighty wind, and it filled all the house where they were sitting. 3) And there appeared unto them cloven tongues like as of fire, and it sat upon each of them. 4) And they were all filled with the Holy Ghost, and began to speak with other tongues, as the Spirit gave them utterance.[37]

Reverend Leonard Lovett of the Church of God in Christ gives a clear definition of Pentecostalism: "It is not a denomination but rather a movement encompassing many denominations, avowedly embracing belief in a Spirit baptism accompanied by various signs, including speaking in tongues."[38]

Walter J. Hollenweger contends that the levels of communication between congregations of Pentecostal churches and other denominations represent the major difference between Pentecostalism and other types of Protestantism. Communication in the Christian world is verbal, whereas the Pentecostal communication "is through a correspondence of sentiments."[39] When the worshipper feels the presence of the spirit they must act on that feeling. Reverend Mercy Dea Thomas states that the Black Pentecostal churches recognize "the three elements of faith which include the intellect, which means to know; the emotion, which means to feel; and the volition, which means to act."[40] Thomas argues that feelings are very important, because the Bible states in St. John 4:24 that "God is a Spirit: and they that worship him must worship him in spirit and in truth."[41] The worship services are highly emotional affairs with "participants speaking in tongues and engaging in ecstatic dancing."[42]

James S. Tinney explains that such fundamentalist Pentecostal churches appeared long before 1906 and were classified as Holiness Churches. Pentecostals accept the experience in Los Angeles as their inauguration because that was the occasion when they acknowledged the experience of speaking in tongues, multitudinous gifts,[43] signs, and manifestations heralding the advent of the Spirit as central to their creed.[44]

The extravagant enthusiasm of Pentecostal ceremonies has its roots in pre-Civil-War Black services, to which freed slaves clung even after they were permitted to attend formerly all-White churches. As David Beckmann points out,

> After the [Civil] War virtually all blacks chose to worship in their own churches, where services were highly emotional, sustained by spirituals and dramatic sermons, often swelling into trance, sometimes climaxing in "holy dance."[45]

They were interested not only in highly emotional services but in freedom of expression. According to Hollenweger,

> They [Blacks] did not believe that God created Africans to be slaves of Europeans. Accordingly, they sang of a God who was involved in history—*their* history—making right what whites have made wrong. . . . Because black people believed that they were God's children, they affirmed their *somebodiness*, refusing to reconcile their servitude with divine revelation.[46]

Freed slaves, still African in origin, were attracted to these "holiness churches," finding solace in the uninhibited expression which was not far from African experiences they had known or heard in the stories of their ancestors.

To better document the freedom experienced in the Black Pentecostal churches, I visited one such church to investigate. I observed services at the Saint Matthew Fire Baptized Holiness Church of God of the Americas in Columbus, Ohio, on Sunday, March 22, 1992.[47] Within the entrance to the church is a foyer and to the left is a massive bulletin board where there were posted announcements of upcoming events for the church, concerts and programs at other churches, and art work from the children's Sunday school classes.

Within the "house of God," there were approximately twenty-five rows of seats sectioned off by two aisles all leading to a raised rostrum with a pulpit. To the left on the main floor area was the musicians' corner. An upright piano was perpendicular to the rostrum with the organ immediately behind it. To the organist's right sat the drummer with an eighteen-piece drum set. He shared the space with a son who played the bongos, another son who played the conga drum, and a daughter who played the maracas. To the left of the organist sat Deacon Marvin Randolph, the bass guitar player. Immediately below the pulpit on the main floor was a table with a deacon standing behind it. (The deacon stood for the entire service.) To the right of the rostrum were six rows of pews for the choir, facing the audience. Above the choir stand was a banner bearing the motto, "The Power of Prayer." Although the church seated approximately two hundred, there were no more than fifty-five members, twenty-five children, and fifteen visitors in attendance. The members were dressed in bright colors with hats, purses, and shoes to match for the ladies and tailored suits with matching handkerchiefs and ties for the men.

Services began at 12:05 p.m. with Deacon Willie Blueford presiding. He began the service with a fast-paced gospel song:

Thank you Lord, Thank You Lord, Thank you Lord for one more day.
Thank you Lord, Thank you Lord, Thank you Lord for one more day.
I want to thank you for being so wonderful, I want to thank you for being so kind,

I want to thank you for waking me up this morning, clothed in my right mind.[48]

His baritone voice was loud and accompanied by his own hand-clapping. One by one all the members of the congregation joined in. Apparently, they knew the song by heart; no one used any hymn books. Deacon Blueford first began a song *a cappella,* and then a pianist began playing. An organist, quickly sat at the organ and began playing, too. Just as quickly her husband began playing the drums; her children started playing the bongos, triangles, and maracas; Deacon Marvin Randolph started playing on the bass guitar; and another musician played the tambourine. Some members were standing, clapping their hands and swaying back and forth to the beat of the music; some were seated, clapping their hands and tapping their feet. The song was sung over and over; there seemed to be no set ending. Blueford was in full control, though, and he finished the song by nodding to the organist, who brought some closure to the fervor of the song and began playing more slowly.

Blueford announced that the worship service was commencing and he began to "outline" the hymn, "A Charge to Keep I Have." To "line out" the hymn, Blueford slowly, and without musical accompaniment, spoke a stanza in a rhythmic staccato beat with a vocal melody, and the congregation repeated the stanza in an upbeat tempo accompanied by the musical instruments. At the end of the stanza they would stop and wait for Blueford to speak another stanza. This continued until, after the last verse of the song, the audience was asked to stand.

Blueford then invited each person to come to the altar to pray. Everyone gathered around the altar, kneeling on cushions before the altar rail and in the surrounding area with eyes closed, and with most speaking out loud: "Lord, Lord," or "Jesus, Jesus, Jesus." I heard expressions such as "Help me, Lord," "Lord, I love you," "Lord, I need you," and "Lord, I thank you," along with recitations of daily blessing. The prayer lasted fifteen minutes and was closed by Blueford speaking very loudly over everyone, "We're going to leave everything in Your hands, a hand that does all things well. These blessings we ask in the name of the Father, the Son, and the Holy Ghost, Amen." At this time everyone stood up and returned to the pews. Some were crying, some saying "Hallelujah," and some saying, "Thank You, Lord."

Rising from his knees, another deacon, Curtis Keaton began singing, "You know I promised the Lord that I would hold out, hold out, hold out; You know I promised the Lord that I would hold out and meet Him in Galilee." During this song, many were doing a holy dance; i.e., shouting to the church members. Which is a charismatic way of jumping up and down, usually very fast, sometimes jumping with two feet and sometimes using one foot at a time, with eyes generally closed and arms, head, and feet moving rhythmically. The musicians were playing throughout the dance. This demonstration was greeted by others saying, "Praise Him," "Hallelujah," "Give the Lord His praise." After about three minutes, those who had started shouting returned to their seats, continuing to say, "Yes," and "Thank You, Jesus," in softer tones than before and during the shouting. As the fervor began to die down, the audience stopped singing and only the musical instruments continued to play. Then Blueford, smiling very broadly, threw up his hands and said, "There ain't no harm in Praising the Lord."

Next Blueford read Psalm 27 from the King James Version of the Bible, and everyone listened attentively. He finished by saying, "May the Lord have a blessing on the reading of His word." He then "testified," telling the audience how good God had been to him all week. After speaking happily of being saved from his sins, sanctified through the truth, and filled with the Holy Ghost and Fire, he declared that he was running for his life and asked the "saints," meaning the congregation, to pray for him. Then he told them to sing their own songs and give their own testimonies about God's goodness to them. Some sang songs and some stood and testified, but all were smiling, standing and swaying during the songs. The testimony service was vibrant, electrifying, and noisy, and filled with more holy dancing and speaking in tongues. Sister Ellen Dinkins rose smiling to give her testimony and began a song:

> Hey, y'all, how've you been doing, Since Jesus came into your heart; Hey, y'all how've you been doing , Since Jesus came into your heart. There's been a great change in me, great change in me; I am so happy, I am so free; There's been a great change in me, great change in me, Since Jesus came into my heart.

I later understood that the song was her an interpretation of the familiar hymn "Since Jesus Came Into My Heart." Dinkins had heard the song a Theresa Goodbread sing it at a convention and the song had been "ringing in her heart since that time." She began her testimony by giving honor to God who was the head of her life, to her pastor, to the saints, to the visitors and to everyone. She spoke of being saved from her sins, sanctified through God's truth, and filled with heaven's Holy Ghost and Fire. Before closing, she asked that those who knew the worth of prayer to pray her strength in the Lord. Small children were present during the services and seemed to enjoy themselves and sang, clapped, played instruments, testified, and even shouted. This part of the service lasted about an hour.

Blueford closed the testimony service when it seemed that everyone was finished. During the offering, everyone stood, and the ushers invited each row of worshippers to walk to the front of the church and deposit offerings in three pans: 1) a public offering; 2) a missionary offering; and 3) consecrated dime for a general offering, located on a table in front of Deacon Blueford. While the congregation walked to the offering table, the musicians played lively music and the congregation began to sing along with them. With the completion of this ceremony, Blueford turned the services over to the pastor, the Reverend Sister Mercy Dea Thomas. She greeted everyone with a smile and began singing,

> When I've lost my direction, You're the compass for my way;
> You're the fiery light, when nights are long and cold;
> In sadness you are the laughter that shadows all my fears;
> When I'm all alone, Your hand is there to hold.
> Jesus, You're the center of my joy, All that's good and perfect comes from you;
> You're the heart of my contentment, Hope for all I do; Jesus, You're the center of my joy.[49]

The pastor gave her testimony in a fiery tone, jumping up and down, with an exuberant "Whooh," and speaking in tongues. She exclaimed, "I love the Lord with all my soul" and professed that she was "glad to be a member of that noisy crowd who loves to shout and praise the Lord." After this she called on the choir, the Voices of Faith, to sing.

Their first number was "Thank you Lord, for all you've done for me," and the second selection was "Let's Praise Him." The soloists of each song stepped to the front and used a microphone. During their songs the soloists emphasized what they were saying by over-articulating phrases and physically demonstrating phrases whenever possible. The director, Sandra Porter, stood in front of the choir using her arms, hands, and fingers as signals to them and to the musician, Alice Williams. While directing, Porter began to dance, turn around, and run slowly up and down the aisles, all to the beat of the music. Both selections were met with enthusiasm from the congregation, who interjected "Amen," "Praise the Lord," "Yes," "Sing, choir," or just "Hallelujah." Many were standing and throwing up their hands, and again there was holy dancing and speaking in tongues.

It was during this high-spirited performance that Pastor Thomas came forth saying, "Hallelujah," and thanked the choir for their selections. She took her text from Psalm 91:14-16[50] and stated that the subject of her sermon was "The Seven I Wills of God." Thomas waited for the congregation to find the scripture and exhorted them always to carry their Bibles (the deacons supplied Bibles to those who did not have them). Upon finding the scripture each member signified the same by standing. When all were standing, they read the scripture in unison. The congregation then sat, and Thomas spoke slowly at first, giving history about the author of the psalm, King David, and about his relationship with God. Afterwards, she began to outline "The Seven I Wills" found in the scripture and interpreted their meaning. She began speaking faster, clapping her hands, throwing her head back, and singing the words in a rhythmic tone. The congregation was continuously responding verbally to the minister: "Preach, Pastor," "Let the Lord use you," "Hallelujah," "Praise the Lord," and "Yes," using the same rhythm established by the pastor. Some called on God personally saying, "Help, Lord," "We need You today," and "Thank You, Jesus."

Thomas preached with great fervor; taking a microphone from its stand, she walked from the pulpit area to the main floor to talk to the congregation, shaking her head constantly and jumping up and down. In one hand, she held the microphone and in the other a large handkerchief which she used to wipe the sweat from her brow. Many times she struck the table with the handkerchiefed hand to emphasize a point. After exclaiming what God would do for them, she began asking the congregation what they would do for God by telling each person to say individually, "I will, Lord," meaning "I will serve You, I will honor You, I will obey You." At one point she put the microphone down and ran up and down the aisles asking member after member, "Can you say, 'Lord, I will'?" The members responded, "I will, Lord." Some began to cry; others were screaming, "Yes, Lord," "Whooh," and "Thank You, Lord."

Two members went to the altar, knelt, and began to cry out to God while the sermon was still in progress. Thomas moved with determination and asked the entire congregation if they felt the Spirit of God. To feel the Spirit, Thomas asked each to stand, close his eyes, hold his hands above his head, and say, "Yes, Lord" from the diaphragm and really mean it. When the worshippers "connected" with God, there was a physical action and/or a verbal response. Some worshippers were crying, holding their head backs and saying "Yes, Lord," some were screaming "Thank You, Lord," others ran around the church, and others performed the holy dance.

Everyone was asked to come to the altar, and those who could not say with assurance, "I will, Lord," were instructed to pray for salvation and to ask God to save them from their sins. After the prayer, which lasted fifteen or twenty minutes, there was another testimony service at the altar for those who were blessed (i.e., who had been healed, who had prayers answered, or who had renewed their willingness to serve the Lord).

One sister acknowledged that she had been burdened but that the Lord had lifted her spirits and she felt light enough to shout some more. One young lady exclaimed that she had backslid—apparently she had committed some sin—and she thanked God for restoring her commitment to Him. The other members were smiling, hugging the sisters, shouting, and saying, "Yes, Lord." The pastor seemed the happiest of all, and after a final prayer the service was dismissed.

To provide closure, Thomas asked each person to "hug someone and tell them you love them." The service ended at 3:15 p.m. but no one seemed to be in a rush to leave. All were hugging, kissing, and speaking about the good service or how good they felt, promising to return for night services at seven o'clock.

AFRICAN ANALOGUES TO PENTECOSTAL RITUALS

As Leonard Lovett points out, Pentecostal rites can be traced to "African and Afro-Caribbean religion."[51] It is no coincidence that African ceremonies and Black Holiness-Pentecostal services both involve sacred dance, spirit possession (called "baptism in the Holy Spirit" within Black Holiness Pentecostalism), call-and-response liturgy, and glossolalia (see below). Melville Herskovits maintains that such "Africanisms" have been freely appropriated by Black Holiness-

Pentecostal churches from pre-slavery African ceremonies preserved in muted form during slavery.[52] Call-and-response worship is found in many churches, of course, but it appears in a far greater number of forms in both African and Pentecostal services than in most other Christian services. During "testimony service," each member stands and gives an account of his day or week, and there is further call and response during the congregational singing, as the deacon outlines the hymn before prayer, and during the sermon of the minister. Glossolalia, a form of "speaking in tongues" is a worshipper's rapid repetition of a word like "Jesus," or "Yes" over and over, faster and faster, until it develops into nonsensical utterances. This suppression of rational thought, a kind of self-induced trance, is regarded as a private conversation between the worshipper and his God. Above all, significant Africanisms in the Pentecostal church include what Lovett calls "a discourse which takes seriously the oral tradition; i. e., testimony, dance, song, spontaneity [which] has merit for Black Holiness-Pentecostalism and the larger culture."[53]

The similarities between Black Pentecostals and African ceremonies have been copiously documented. Pentecostal holy dances, writes William Clark, bear "a close resemblance to some of the primitive tribal dances of Central and West Coast Africa. They are not typical plantation Negro dances nor are they any of the stage forms which the writer has observed."[54] Other Africanisms found in the Pentecostal rites have to do with the instruments and musical accompaniment used in their churches. First, Simpson points out that musical accompaniment can be provided by hand-clapping and foot-stamping as well as with every known type of percussion instrument. "In this church," he writes,

> No hymnals are used; the songs are spirituals; and the rhythm is emphasized in the singing through the use of drums and tambourines, as well as the stamping of feet and the clapping of hands. The spiritual and the related contemporary Gospel music have long communicated Biblical themes in black American communities.[55]

James Tinney, in arguing for the Black roots of all Pentecostal worship, supports his case thus:

Many have observed that the percussive sounds that fill the air in charismatic services are importations from Africa. Although the timbrel or small hand drum is mentioned in Scripture, extensive use of drums is a contribution of black Pentecostalism. As James Baldwin has pointed out, the drum is the indispensable Africanism in Pentecostal worship, and shuffling and dancing are in its convoy, along with highly emotionalized motor reactions, including ecstatic tongues.[56]

Many instruments brought from Africa are still included in the Pentecostal churches. Excluded from the services of many other churches as "noise-makers," the drum and tambourine are necessary church instruments for Pentecostals. Others include the piano and/or organ, the guitar, maracas, bongos, the xylophone, the triangle, and a small washing board played with a tablespoon. In addition to awakening reverence, the instruments are used to punctuate the minister's sermons, and to provide harmonious accompaniment for those who are shouting or speaking in tongues.

Speaking in tongues, as it is known to most African-Americans, is one of the most unusual aspects of Pentecostal worship, and one of obvious African lineage. It is known to most Africans as a "trance experience," which David Beckmann defines as "an altered state of consciousness accompanied by agitation or activity."[57] In the church "speaking in tongues" is not a scheduled part of the liturgy but rather a spontaneous outburst which is respected and honored. It appears as a private conversation between the worshipper and his God. In some cases the worshipper, rather than speaking to God, receives a message from Him. At these times either that worshipper or another one may interpret the tongues for the congregation. If not, the congregation remains unaware of the tenor of the "conversation."

In America, trance is a relatively private experience practiced by a small group of charismatics. Most Pentecostals, for instance confine "speaking in tongues" to the privacy of their homes and to churches where this practice is understood. Primarily, this is due to the negative stigma attached to this procedure by those who do not understand it. In Africa, however, as Margaret and Henry Drewal record, the trance experience, accepted and practiced by the majority, is fully public and even theatrical; that is, it requires an audience.[58]

Despite this difference—attributable to the different cultural mores of the two continents or (as Beckmann suggests), to the influence of "St. Paul's advice in 1 Corinthians 14: 18, 19"[59]—Beckmann insists on the African origin of the trance component of Pentecostal worship:

> Although the development of Afro-Pentecostal churches has been largely independent, they originated from Pentecostal missions. Trance was derived from African religion, but the biblical argument which allows for it in Christian worship, C. F. Parhams' innovation, was carried back to Africa and Afro-Americans in the Caribbean by missionaries.[60]

Another African legacy through which Pentecostal worshippers achieve heightened spirituality—a means of inducing a kind of communal trance—is the ritual component of their services. Ritual is frequently defined as the observation of set forms and ceremonies as a part of public worship. The key terms in this definition are "set" and "public." The effect of the following set forms is to remove the worshipper from mental habits used in the mundane tasks of day-to-day living: making plans, taking positions, defining, analyzing, criticizing—in short, the whole spectrum of self-conscious ratiocination that establishes an individual's autonomy. The very familiarity of the words and actions of a ritual anesthetizes these faculties so that deeper levels of awareness may awaken, giving rise to spirituality.

It is for this reason that strangers to any ritual often find it comical: unfamiliar with it, they cling to their autonomy, unable to lose themselves in the ceremony. Equally important is the public nature of ritual. Trance, as we have seen, may be public or private, but ritual by its very nature is a communal experience. Sharing this trance experience stimulates a spiritual mode of thought and feeling, thereby achieving several goals: inner peace, self-affirmation, acceptance, and "belonging." Understood in this way, Pentecostal ritual appears to Robert Williams as "A potent form of action. . . . As the most important phenomenon of religion, ritual is an orderly means by which one participates in the simulation, and sometimes the investigation, of reality."[61]

Thus, any successful ritual offers the worshippers a momentary retreat from the pain of individuality. Ritual, then, provides an opportunity for a group to order events with full participation by all members. The perspective provided by such an experience might enable one to solve problems that previously seemed hopeless. After defining ritual, Williams explains its purpose not only in religion but in the everyday existence of Afro-Americans:

> Within black religion, as expressed in its African and Afro-American forms, ritual is almost always associated with moral conflict and social problems. The salvation or resolution, which comprises the goal of ritual practice, relates to human conflict and social problems.[62]

YORUBA RITUALISTIC PRACTICES

The purpose of ritual among the Yoruba is very similar to that of ritual in Black Pentecostal religion. In order to deal with problems of daily life, Williams explains:

> Among the Yoruba people of Nigeria, . . . the orishas, or gods, are numerous, and as such, they act *via* ritual practice to order human life. . . . Ritual, as in the Ifa divination of the Yoruba, invokes a sacred time through which assistance from a god is used to handle ordinary concerns and problems.[63]

Close examination of certain African rituals having counterparts in the Black Pentecostal church and the National Black Theatre will demonstrate the social dilation of individual consciousness which ritual provides. Since my ultimate purpose in illustrating the African origins of Pentecostal forms of worship is to trace the ancestry of certain features of Teer's National Black Theatre, I will examine ritual among the Yoruba tribe that Teer herself visited and from whom she borrowed consciously and directly, as well as indirectly through the Pentecostal influences on her theatre and its productions.

According to Brenda Cotto-Escalera, "The Yoruba is one of the largest ethnic groups in West Africa" and "can be found in southwestern Nigeria, in a section of the Bendel state of Nigeria, and in the Republics of Togo and Benin,"[64] less than one hundred miles southeast of Oshogbo. She also writes that "A great number of the slaves brought to the Americas were of Yoruba origin. There are large concentrations of Yoruba descendents all over America, particularly in the Caribbean, Brazil, and the United States."[65]

With many American slaves being of Yoruba origin, much of this tradition has been passed on and continues to be perpetuated, as can be seen in the many similarities between current Pentecostal ceremonies and ancient rituals of the Yoruba. Michael O'Brien, a former resident of Nigeria, remarks that most "Yoruba I know, when converting from Muslimism, convert to the Pentecostal religion because they find a strong kinship within that form of worship."[66]

In the early 1970s Teer met Ulli Beier, a German who was head of the African Studies program at the University of Ife in Nigeria. He came to the theatre dressed in his dashiki and African sandals and confided to Teer that her theatre reminded him of rituals he had attended in Africa. He spoke of the beauty of Africa and especially the deity of the Oshun near the village of Oshogbo. Beier helped Teer obtain a Ford Fellowship to visit Africa and gave her a letter of introduction to the king at Oshogbo.[67]

Visiting Nigeria in 1972, Teer was especially inspired by the rituals practiced in this village, sensing a link between them and her supposed ancestors. It was here that Teer found the elements which solidified her feelings about African theatrical elements. According to Beier, "popular Yoruba theatre developed from church moralities,"[68] and Teer learned that

> Oshogbo has a reputation in Yorubaland as a town of peace. The town has never been known to play a leading part in aggressive wars and it has been extremely lucky in that during the protracted tribal wars of the eighteenth and nineteenth centuries Oshogbo was never conquered by enemies.[69]

The reason for the town's good fortune has not been explained, but it is certainly not because Oshogbo is a small village or lacks enviable resources, for, as Beier continues, "Oshogbo is a big trading center, a market town, rich and self-confident.[70]

Teer discovered that in Oshogbo artists are important people who have titles and positions of importance. Teer was interested in this custom, which runs counter to Western traditions that place importance on scientists, mathematicians, and engineers. Whereas Westerners value professionals who apply their creativity to "useful" and "practical" ends, these Africans believe that creative artists give them reason to rise from their beds, thus serving the most useful and practical of all possible functions.

Teer also found inspiration in African religious festivals. She writes: "I found strong similarities between African rituals and the black American 'Holy roller' church. If you go to Africa, you see the same forms that you see in the church, the elements of ritual— preaching rhythms, dance, music, chants."[71] She saw similarities between the African ritual services and the services at the Pentecostal churches she had visited in Harlem, and she saw how both resembled the type of theatre she had been performing at the National Black Theatre. She felt that she was at home.

The religious festivals of Oshogbo center upon the town's patroness deity, who is, according to Beier,

> the important water goddess Osun [also spelled Oshun]. Osun is the
> 'Orisha" [holy power] to whom women pray for children. She is
> known and loved for her power to produce fertility and prosperity
> everywhere where Yoruba live.[72]

According to Susanne Wenger, "Every town or settlement is crowned by one outstandingly important divine-ancestral celebration, like the Osun festival in Oshogbo."[73] In Yoruba tradition, Osun is the goddess of riches, beauty, harmony, and love. She is the deity of fertility incarnated as the river Oshun. Many people believe that Oshun's spirit now lives in the river, and they come from all over the world to renew their spirits and rejuvenate their bodies by walking in Her sacred groves and washing in Her abundant waters. This becomes a

form of worship for the Yoruba "which demands creativity and
pleasure in handling symbols. Symbolic action brings the worshipper
into the very depths of magic procedures in creation, and gives him
freedom also to fly up into the cool abstractions of mystic
adventures."[74]

Wenger also reports that the Yoruba "still celebrate thirteen major
traditional festivals each year. The most important are: the Oshun
festival . . . the festival of Shango . . . the Egungun festival . . . and the
Ifa Festival."[75] In Oshogbo, the Osun Festival takes place for two
weeks each August and includes the all-night festival of sixteen lamps,
the Oshun River Festival, and Oriki Day. Beier writes that "To witness
the Osun festival or to visit the holy river and holy groves in the forest
nearby is for the worshippers not only a joyful event but also an
emotional experience which turns them bodily and spiritually fertile."[76]
The festivals are special events, and visitors come daily to wash in the
waters and pray to Oshun. There are also private celebrations practiced
by the worshippers; and according to Beier,

> Though the music, dancing and poetry that belong to this ancient
> culture are still very much alive, Oshogbo has at the same time
> become a centre for contemporary artistic activities. It is this lively
> existence side by side of different cultural activities, the complex
> stratification and integration of classical-traditional, popular-naieve,
> and sophisticated-modern art forms, that makes Oshogbo such a
> lively and exciting town.[77]

Whether coming for the festival or just paying a daily visit,
worshippers must, according to Beier, view their stay at Oshogbo as an
emotional experience. The degree to which they give themselves over
to their feelings will determine their degree of satisfaction with the
experience and the fulfillment they achieve. Exposure to this culture
confirmed Teer's growing conviction that feelings were the key to self-
knowledge and fulfillment.

Teer was also struck by the Yoruba's sincere reverence for their
gods. Coming from a culture which believed in one God, she at first felt
distanced from much of the ceremony. Yet she was drawn in by the

sincerity of the worshippers. Her experience, according to Wenger, is common:

> As to the serene beauty of ritual, no one has witnessed it without being involved and part of it. As to the conjuring rhythm of song and recitation and attributive addresses, no one can grasp the message without previous sequences of initiations into the capacities of multidimensional experiences.[78]

Wenger adds that each observer or participant becomes involved in the services, a circumstance that echoes the call and response of the Pentecostal church, and the use of audience involvement in Teer's plays.

The single feature common among Yoruba tradition, Pentecostal worship, and NBT performances, is communion, or the absorption of the self into a larger community through the suppression of reason and the stimulation of deeper centers of awareness and attention. Wenger explains this spiritual experience thus:

> Religious thought is multi-dimensional, is beyond time and outside rational means. Religious instinct is energized from mankind's psychic nucleus which projects its magnified shadow onto the horizons of our universe. From this nucleus of life itself a culture's originality emerges, from these it branches into expression, detailed by ritual and art, which too vibrate, out from emotional strings, roots which vibrate with the vibrations of life's continuous beginnings, which are rhythm.[79]

The physical expressions of religion, according to Wenger, cannot always be explained because their roots are centered in the heart and soul of a people. Each culture establishes a rhythm, and this rhythm vibrates with its own unique beat. This was a theory with which Teer and her company identified, for from rhythm came the roots of life, the emotions, the culture's originality, and its religious instincts. "The people of Oshogbo were highly spirited," reported Ade Faison, a member of Teer's theatre who has also been to Oshogbo many times. After viewing the performance, he added that,

The Babalawo [spiritual leader] danced on rocks and gravel barefooted in a magic ceremony. And also during the all-night celebration there were many lights from bulbs and candles. The highlight of the evening was the emergence of the King, who danced around the lights three times to invoke the will of the Gods for a prosperous year.[80]

Teer was drawn to this town and became a part of it. She has returned every year since 1972 to Oshogbo to be restored. What most impressed Teer in Yoruba culture was the value of the arts. The rituals performed are centered on the gifts of the artists and performers.

Of the manifold Yoruba traditions, the Gelede performances, common to nearly all Yoruba, provide a convenient focus for my study. The Gelede are ritualistic "performances carefully conceived and executed to pay homage to women so that the community may partake of their innate power for its benefit."[81] According to the Drewals, the

Gelede began in the latter part of the eighteenth century among the Ketu Yoruba, spreading rapidly to other Yoruba groups and, as a consequence of the nineteenth-century Atlantic slave trade, to the dispersed Yoruba of Sierra Leone, Cuba, and Brazil.[82]

The Gelede performances have become widely known and have the following characteristics. Foremost is the plentiful use of spectacle. Gelede ritual has been called "the ultimate spectacle for its ability to shape society and to create a lasting impression by means of an absorbing multimedia experience . . . by singers, dancers, carvers, drummers, and spectators. It appeals to the senses through a brilliant array of sounds, sights, and energy."[83] These passionate performances are divided into two parts, the first being "Efe," which is "a night of songs," during which "performers [are] dramatically attired and are constantly in motion."[84] Each performer enters the performance area singly, with each entrance more spectacular than the last, culminating with the entrance of the Oro Efe, costumed, singing, and dancing. His movement embodies "stateliness and grandeur" as he "communicates overt masculine power and authority, the authority that comes from the mothers' support."[85]

The second part of the Gelede ritual comes on the following afternoon, when the "spectacle is created by an integration of masks, costumes, music, and dance."[86] Continuing well into the night, the performance is a collage of pageantry including colorful costumes and masks.

An important similarity between the Gelede and the rituals of Black Pentecostals is the interaction between the performers and the audience. Just as in Pentecostal churches call-and-response practices erase the distinction between minister and congregation, so this inclusion of the audience in the performance seems to be almost the *raison d'etre* of Gelede. As the Drewals explain this phenomenon:

> Performance implies a separation between actor and audience, both in distance and in distinction, maintained by means of a masquerade format. Yet in the course of Gelede the lines between performer and audience blur as enthralled spectators become active participants. This process of inclusion and participation is precisely the ultimate goal and meaning of the ritual, for its fundamental purpose is to honor the mothers from whom we all come.[87]

To facilitate this interaction between performers and audience, the Yoruba induce a "ritually transcendent state" by the use of the drums, "and at the close a 'cooling' rite is performed to restore [the audience] to normalcy."[88] Thus, the ecstatic trance, as in Pentecostal ceremonies, is a vital component of Yoruba ceremonies. One illustration is a "possession trance, when during ceremonies the gods become manifest in the world in the bodies of their devotees. Other examples of temporary manifestations of the supernatural occur in the masquerade performances of ancestral spirits, Egungun, and in Gelede."[89]

The social interaction of Gelede rituals contains divine presences, which serve to ratify the value system implicit in the myths which the ceremonies celebrate. Gelede performances are ultimately instructive, according to the Drewals: "Gelede serves a didactic function as it reinforces social values and traditions. Values are enforced with reference to particular individuals or groups, or sometimes they are asserted in general terms."[90]

And yet, for all the emphasis on community in Gelede performances, and although there is an order of service or program, there is still room for spontaneity. In the Gelede, "The drummers may launch spontaneously into a verbal/rhythmic text associated with a visual motif" during the night of songs, and "since the identity of the dancer is generally known, his name may be sounded and incorporated into the rhythm."[91] Such spontaneity shows that the drummers and dancers are polished and secure in their performance, and so are able to extemporize in such a celebration.

In short, then, there are a number of similarities between the Black Pentecostal church services and the Gelede performances of the Yoruba. They both involve lavish dress; both use musical instruments, drummers, and dancers; both employ trance and/or trance-like states, a call-and-response technique involving audience participation, and a certain element of individuality.

Turning to the National Black Theatre, many of the same elements can be found. Teer was inexperienced in theatrical theory, Black Pentecostalism, and Yoruba traditions, and so she turned by instinct to her inner feelings and her cultural heritage. Genevieve Fabre offers one explanation for the course taken by Teer and others:

> The drama traditionally written by whites requires catharsis [as specified by Aristotle], whereas the ideology of revolutionary theatre established more critical reflection. By refusing catharsis, black theatre does not renounce its emotive function, but adds exercise to exorcism. In the best performances . . . reflection stems from emotions and creates the effect of shock. Emotion is not an end in itself but a means to construct meaning.[92]

Beginning in 1968, Teer began to experiment, using her emotions to guide her theatre's ideology. Dissatisfied with Western traditional theatre, she decided to invent a theatre which could satisfy her.

Teer at once seized upon the ritualistic practices of Pentecostals and Africans as a starting point, partly because of their innate theatricality, "integrating," as Fabre puts it, "musical forms, narrative, and choreography specific to Black culture."[93] Teer stated that "You can't put that magic in a play," for "plays are nothing but ego trips, anyway, you stand up there on stage reciting lines, and the audience flips out because you've mastered an acting technique."[94] But to Teer a ritual was different because it was

> A holy experience; you deal with a congregation of people. A ritual is a family affair. In a ritual you mend and heal the mental wounds in the minds of your people. You attempt to get your people out of the box that Western civilization has placed us in, inhibiting us, keeping us from being natural. You wash away all negative Western thought patterns, because essentially a ritual concerns itself with decrudding.[95]

Teer wanted her rituals to be works which concentrated on raising consciousness. To this end, Mance Williams reports that the "NBT coined the term ritualistic revivals to describe what they did." He defines it thus:

> The ritual part is a musical experience of overpowering creative force that entertains and transforms the audience. Combined in these rituals are elements of religion, dance, music, incantation, and the communal experience. The revival side expresses and celebrates the joy of living and provides for both performers and spectators a liberating catharsis.[96]

Teer's aim was not, however, to take the African and Pentecostal rituals literally in order to change the behavior of African-Americans, for she does not, according to James Hatch,

> impose Yoruba rituals on Black Americans, but rather develop[s] eclectic forms based on close examination of Black life in America with its intuitive and acquired rhythms and rituals of the street, church, bar, school, and family. All offer form, content, and style that can be used to raise the consciousness of Afro-Americans as to who they are, and who they can be.[97]

Teer declared that she wanted a theatre where the audience and performers might have the same electrifying experiences as she had witnessed in the Pentecostal churches of Harlem. Her first trip to Africa in 1972 acquainted her with African rituals, which she related to the practices of Black Pentecostals, confirming her decision to include such elements in her theatre.

The main element that excited Teer's imagination was ritual. Bruce McConachie, whose theory of cultural hegemony was cited in Chapter I, applies that theory when he describes a ritual as a

> Repetitious, formalized, and dramatically-structured communication of significant cultural meanings, effected through the involvement and catharsis of its participants, which functions to legitimate an image of a social order. The "dramatically-structured elements" may vary widely from ritual to ritual, but include music, song, call-response, liturgical chanting, dance, impersonation, incarnation, story—in sum, theatrical elements.[98]

From the Pentecostal Churches and the Yoruba rituals, Teer borrowed theatrical elements with which she felt comfortable, those ingredients which separated her from white culture. In music these included rhythms familiar to Black Americans, in the cadences of jazz, blues, soul, spiritual, and gospel. Teer employed African drummers for every acting training session as well as for performances. The speech of performances was likewise modeled on that used in Harlem churches: the so-called Black English common among Blacks throughout the country, although American standard English was not wholly eschewed, it is upon these theatrical elements that Teer launched her theory of a theatre that culminated in the National Black Theatre of Harlem.

Performances also included "testimony" from the audience and cast, consisting of impromptu personal anecdotes about how they had overcome some difficulty. During testimony, auditors offered support with comments such as "You can make it," "I'm a witness," "He brought me through," and "I know God cares about you." This sudden intimacy between perfect strangers—escalating after the performance into hugs, kisses, prayers, and even offers of money—was Teer's goal. Just as sharing personal travails and accomplishments in church enables the congregation to greet one another familiarly as "sister" or "brother" before they become fully acquainted, the same activity in a theatre creates a bond of fellow-feeling that is known as "the ensemble effect."

Teer's adaptation of the call-and-response aspect of religious services was governed by an unwritten code of taste which, while welcoming spontaneous outbursts by all parties and the use of intimate phrases expressing solidarity, prevented demonstrations from becoming unruly.

Nevertheless, from the point of view of many White spectators, these elements of Pentecostal worship and Yoruba rituals appear comic or incredible in a theatre. The reasons for this reaction are not obvious, and since Teer feels this element of her theatre calls deeply to Black people, it deserves investigation. The culture-shock many Whites experience at an NBT production is due in part to their self-enforced isolation from Black culture, in worship as well as in daily chores. Living in a hegemonic society necessitates disguise in order to succeed or even to exist, so Blacks learn White ways in their efforts to adapt; but Whites almost never have occasion to observe, and even less likely to understand, Black life. However, the patronizing or even hostile reaction of Whites may have more deep-seated causes, for when Pentecostalism first started Blacks and Whites worshipped together and therefore had sufficient exposure to each other's culture to make for familiarity. Yet Black and White Pentecostals eventually separated all the same. Among the reasons cited by Lovett, were the highly emotional services Blacks favored—especially the holy dancing—the somewhat "wordly" music Blacks preferred, and what amounted to outright racism: some Whites did not want to hear Blacks either offering testimonies or preaching.[99]

Although this historical episode offers no evidence of any basic temperamental difference between the races, it seems clear enough that Blacks in general can tolerate more enthusiasm than can Whites. It is this difference that Teer exploited in borrowing from Pentecostal services and Yoruba rituals, those elements that not only fostered a healthy familiarity among cast and audience, but also set Blacks apart as a coherent and sharply defined subculture. These included the elements of dance, call and response, testimony service, musical instruments, highly emotionalized motor reactions, speaking in tongues, and respect for verbal and physical spontaneous outbursts.

Upon these theatrical elements Teer based her theory of theatre that culminated in the NBT of Harlem.

NOTES

1. Barbara Ann Teer, "Reinvention of a People," *Amsterdam News*, 22 December 1984, 13.

2. Teer, "Reinvention of a People," 13.

3. Clifton F. Brown, "Black Religion—1968," *In Black America* (Los Angeles, California: Presidential Publishers, 1970), p. 183.

4. *Who's Who Among Black Americans, Inc.* 1st ed., ed. William C. Matney (Northbrook, Illinois: Publishing Co., 1976) vol. 1, 610.

5. Larry Bivins, "Success without Compromise," *Newsday*, 14 April 1988, 24.

6. Bivins, 24.

7. Bivins, 24.

8. Bivins, 24.

9. Quoted in Gary Schoichet, "Barbara Ann Teer," *Other Stages*, 17 April 1980, 2.

10. Private interview, 24 October 1987.

11. Schoichet, 2.

12. Private interview, 24 October 1987.

13. Private interview, 24 October 1987.

14. Edward Mapp, *Directory of Blacks in the Performing Arts* (Metuchen, N.J.: The Scarecrow Press, Inc., 1978), p. 356.

15. Barbara Ann Teer, "The Great White Way Is Not *Our* Way—Not Yet," *Negro Digest*, April 1968, 25.

16. Charlie L. Russell, "Barbara Ann Teer: We Are Liberators Not Actors," *Essence* (March, 1971), 49.

17. Russell, 50.

18. Valerie Harris, "Power Exchange 2: Barbara Ann Teer," in *Third World Women: The Politics of Being Other*, vol. 2 (New York: Heresies Collective, Inc., 1979), 42-43

19. "Barbara Ann Teer and The National Black Theatre," *Interreligious Foundation for Community Organization News*, Jan.-Feb., 1972, 1.

20. Barbara Ann Teer, Personal interview, 24 October 1987.

21. Quoted in Larry Bivins, "Success Without Compromise," 24.

22. Teer, *Negro Digest*, 29.

23. Teer, *Negro Digest*, 28.

24. Teer, *Negro Digest*, 28.

25. Ruby Dee, "The Tattered Queens," in *The International Library of Negro Life and History Anthology of the American Negro in the Theatre*, 2nd ed., ed. Lindsay Patterson, (New York, Washington, London: Publishers Company, Inc., 1969),135.

26. Sandy Satterwhite, "Black Actress Shares Her Soul," *New York Post* 6 February 1976, 21.

27. Valerie Harris, 42.

28. Teer interview, 27 October 1992.

29. Phone conversation, March 1986.

30. Teer, *Negro Digest*, 27.

31. Valerie Harris, 43.

32. Jessica B. Harris, "The National Black Theatre: The Sun People of 125th Street," in *The Theatre of Black Americans*, ed. Errol Hill (New York: Applause, 1987), 286.

33. George Eaton Simpson, "Black Pentecostalism in the United States," *Phylon* vol. 35, no. 2, 203.

34. Reverend Leonard Lovett, "The Spiritual Legacy and Role of Black Holiness-Pentecostalism in the Development of American Culture," *One in Christ*, vol. 23 no. 142 (1987),149.

35. Simpson, 203.

36. Malcolm J. C. Calley, *God's People: West Indian Pentecostal Sects in England* (London: Cambridge University Press, 1965), p. 12.

37. *The Holy Bible*, King James Version (Nashville: Holman Bible Publishers, 1979), p. 78.

38. Lovett, 144.

39. W. J. Hollenweger, *The Pentecostals: The Charismatic Movement in the Churches* (Minneapolis: Augsburg, 1972), p. xviii.

40. Private phone conversation, 21 July 1992.

41. *Holy Bible*, p. 90.

42. Simpson, 206.

43. These spiritual gifts are according to 1 Corinthians 12: 4-11, which states: "4) Now there are diversities of gifts, but the same Spirit. 5)And there are differences of administrations, but the same Lord. 6)And there are diversities of operations, but it is the same God which worketh all in all. 7) But the

manifestation of the Spirit is given to every man to profit withal. 8) For to one is given by the Spirit the word of wisdom; to another the word of knowledge by the same Spirit: 9) To another faith by the same Spirit; to another the gifts of healing by the same Spirit: 10) To another the working of miracles: to another prophecy; to another discerning of spirits; to another *divers* kinds of tongues; to another the interpretation of tongues: 11) But all these worketh that one and the selfsame Spirit, dividing to every man severally as he will."

44. James S. Tinney, "Black Origins of the Pentecostal Movement," *Christianity Today*, vol. 16 (October 8, 1971), 5.

45. David M. Beckmann, "Trance from Africa to Pentecostalism," *Concordia Theological Monthly*, vol. 45, no. 1 (January 1974), 20.

46. Walter J. Hollenweger, "Pentecostalism and Black Power," *Theology Today*, vol. 30, no. 3 (October, 1973), 232.

47. In my professional opinion of Pentecostal church services, the Sunday morning services of St. Matthew represents the typical services at most Black holiness churches including Church of God in Christ, Apostolic, Church of the Firstborn, Church of the Living God, and the Church of God Pillar and Ground of Truth.

48. Composer Unknown. This song is known as a congregational song, usually composed by members of the denomination and sung at an inspired moment when God has blessed them. This happens frequently. The musicians, who know how to play by ear, accompany the songster's singing and rhythm. The audience follows along and the song is sung over and over until the congregation feels comfortable. Some songs are also composed by the members from biblical scriptures.

49. Originally recorded by The Richard Smallwood Singers.

50. "Because he hath set his love upon me, therefore will I deliver him: I will set him on high, because he hath known my name. He shall call upon Me, and I will answer him: I will be with him in trouble; I will deliver him, and honour him. With long life will I satisfy him, and shew him My salvation."

51. Lovett, 145.

52. Melville J. Herskovits, *The Myth of the Negro Past* (New York: Harper & Brothers, 1940), p. 231.

53. Lovett, 155.

54. William A. Clark, "Sanctification in Negro Religion," *Social Forces* vol. 15, no. 4 (May 1937), 547-548.

55. Simpson, 206.

56. Tinney, 5.

57. Beckmann, p. 11.

58. Henry John Drewal and Margaret Thompson Drewal, *Gelede: Art and Power among the Yoruba* (Bloomington, Indiana: Indiana University Press, 1983), p. 2.

59. Beckmann, p. 13. 1 Corinthians 14: 18-19 states, "I thank God, I speak with tongues more than ye all: Yet in the church I had rather speak five words with my understanding, that *by my voice* I might teach others also, than ten thousand word in an *unknown* tongue."

60. Beckmann, 24.

61. Robert C. Williams, "Ritual, Drama, and God in Black Religion: Theological and Anthropological Views." *Theology Today*, vol. 41, no. 4 (January 1985), 433.

62. Williams, 434.

63. Williams, 435-436.

64. Brenda L. Cotto-Escalera, "Masks, Performance Traditions, and Cultural Diversity: Exploring African Culture through African Masks," *Theatre and Education Youth Theatre Journal*, vol. 5, no. 4, (1991): 10.

65. Cotto-Escalera, 10.

66. Personal interview with Michael O'Brien, Thursday, 17 December 1992. O'Brien was a student in my Introduction to Theatre Honor Class, Fall, 1992. His parents are non-denominational missionaries in Nigeria, West Africa, and he is familiar with the Ibadan and Benin areas which lie very close to Oshogbo. O'Brien lived in Nigeria for ten years.

67. Personal interview (June 24, 1992) with Tunde Samuel, National Black Theatre Production Coordinator, who has been with Teer since 1971.

68. Ulli Beier, *The Sacred Art of Susanne Wenger* (London: Cambridge University Press, 1975), p. 22.

69. Beier, p. 20.

70. Beier, p. 6.

71. Larry Bivins, "Success Without Compromise," *Newsday* 14 April 1988, 24.

72. Beier, p. 6.

73. Susanne Wenger, *The Timeless Mind of the Sacred, Its New Manifestation in the Osun Grove* (Oshogbo: Institute of African Studies, University of Ibadan, Adeyemo Press, 1977), p. 31. Wenger is accepted as the major authority on Oshogbo; she is the only White who was accepted sufficiently to live for years

in the village and who is allowed to sculpt gods in the groves of the Osun River. She has written several texts on the subject.

74. Beier, p. 17.

75. Beier, p. 19.

76. Beier, p. 7.

77. Beier, pp. 19-20.

78. Wenger, p. 31.

79. Wenger, p. 12.

80. Personal interview with Ade Faison at the National Black Theatre, 25 June 1992; viewed video, also.

81. Henry John Drewal and Margaret Thompson Drewal, *Gelede: Art and Power among the Yoruba* (Bloomington, Indiana: Indiana University Press, 1983), p. xv.

82. Drewal and Drewal, p. xv.

83. Drewal and Drewal, p. 12.

84. Drewal and Drewal, p. 12

85. Drewal and Drewal, p. 12.

86. Drewal and Drewal, pp. 12-13.

87. Drewal and Drewal, p. 14.

88. Drewal and Drewal, p. 4.

89. Drewal and Drewal, p. 2.

90. Drewal and Drewal, p. 13.

91. Drewal and Drewal, p. 13.

92. Genevieve Fabre, *Drums, Masks, and Metaphor*, Trans. Melvin Dixon (Cambridge, Massachusetts: Harvard University Press, 1988), p. 241.

93. Fabre, p. 230.

94. Quoted in Russell, 50.

95. Quoted in Russell, 50.

96. Mance Williams, *Black Theatre in the 1960s and 1970s: A Historical-Critical Analysis of the Movement* (Westport, Connecticut: Greenwood Press, 1985), p. 51.

97. James V. Hatch, "Some African Influences on the Afro-American Theatre," in *The Theatre of Black Americans*, ed. Errol Hill (New York: Applause, 1987), 21.

98. Bruce McConachie, "Towards a Postpositivist Theatre History," *Theatre Journal*, vol. 37 (1985), 474-475.

99. Lovett, 147-149.

III
The National Black Theatre: The Beginning

No longer AM I the little me
I AM no longer the small me
No longer AM I the separate me
I AM no longer the different me
I AM free, free, to be who I was born to be
ONE with my family.

Barbara Ann Teer, NBT, 1991

Launching a new theatre in 1968 did not seem unusual, for many non-traditional theatres were being founded around this time. However, Teer's theatrical theory was revolutionary and radical. She also formulated a scientific approach to her goals and objectives, articulating a vision in a well-written, well-organized plan.

This chapter will focus on the beginning of the National Black Theatre, and on its goals and their implementation. The concept of "soul," which is the basis of Teer's ideology, will also be examined. To explain Teer's need for developing the NBT and to discover the foundation for the NBT classes, I will consider first some differences between Afrocentric and Eurocentric values.

Important differences in thinking habits, learning styles, and social behavior have caused difficulties in the schooling of some Blacks. Linda Myers asserts that

The first step in our move toward pluralism must be based on critical
self-evaluation in an effort to gain sincere acceptance and
appreciation of self. Once one has truly come to understand and value
self, any fear of the unknown or the unfamiliar should diminish. . . .
If, on the other hand, self-knowledge does not lead to a basic sense of
security and well-being, fear of the unfamiliar will increase. Negative
beliefs regarding difference will become more deeply entrenched.
Individuals and societies will create barriers in an attempt to protect
their unexamined sense of themselves.[1]

The process of understanding self becomes more difficult in an
environment where unsympathetic teachers are trying to teach an
African-American who he and/or she is. Yet there is a great deal of
every African-American's identity of which he is only subliminally
aware—and much more that his teachers, particularly his White
teachers, may not prize even if they do recognize its existence. Speech,
bodily movements, eyelid motions, laughter, learning styles—these and
many other mannerisms are important links between every African-
American and his cultural past. Myers offers one example of a different
learning method in writing that

African-American students . . . perform best when multiple stimuli
are presented simultaneously. . . . learning exercises incorporating
visual and auditory stimuli and involving motor activity would be
preferable for African-American students, while sitting quietly
working on math problems or reading may be more appropriate for
Euro-American children.[2]

James Anderson writes that Blacks use few synonyms or comparisons,
and tend to use the second person "you" to reflect group identity, and
often choose words more for their emotional content than for their strict
denotations.[3]

    Although Blacks have lived in a Eurocentric environment, they
still retain many of their Africanisms. Anderson records that

A significant number of African behaviors, values, and beliefs have
been carried over by contemporary Blacks. These survived because

of the existence of institutions such as the Black church and the Black family. Probably a more significant explanation is that one's entire cultural style does not have to change because some behaviors are borrowed from the dominant culture.[4]

However, biculturality can be a source of confusion for African-Americans who cannot decide which style to adopt to define cultural identity. "Code switching" permits superficial participation in both cultures, but building a sense of identity requires a permanent choice at a deep level. Confusion arises from the fact that most African-Americans know more about being American than being African, and they do not fully understand the rewards of their dual heritage. A free choice of decisions based on being African or American can only be made on the basis of adequate knowledge and without duress. However, African-Americans have often been forced to choose in relative ignorance, aware that success in society will depend on making the "right" choice—or the White choice. Myers reports that

Although great strides have been made in the reclamation of their heritage, there are many African-Americans who have yet to learn the truth about their cultural ancestry. Still other African- Americans have been so affected by the racist brainwashings they receive daily, they do not want to identify with African culture.[5]

Many Black children, according to Myers, attend public institutions where they are taught about Eurocentric culture rather than their own. Although some institutions have begun teaching African-American history, in most cases the accomplishments of Blacks are taught to the exclusion of other elements of their culture. Even then, Black history is taught only as a separate unit and for a few students. For the most part, Black students are taught Eurocentric precepts, learning styles, and habits of speech; even the foods eaten during lunchtime are Eurocentric. When a Black family does not attend a Black church, the problem grows; and it only compounds itself when a student who has working parents or a single working parent tries to embrace his own roots.

If all Black students learned well what they are taught, the problem would be lessened; they would gain a cultural heritage, even if not "their own." But a child who knows he is "different," whether or not he is aware of and proud of what makes him different, does not always find it easy to absorb the cultural indoctrination the schools afford. There are, of course, many Blacks who have fully assimilated White culture, but there are a great many who, for many reasons, cannot do so—because they lack the ability or have invested too much of themselves in their own half-understood culture, or they lack a burning desire to "succeed" in the White world at any cost. These are the Blacks whom our educational system does not serve well.

Teer has stated that what is needed is "a massive cultural and artistic movement to make people culturally literate." The people she is trying to reach, ultimately, are those "who don't even know what culture is, who don't even respect art, who think it's some luxury or some leisure or some little thing that you do in your spare time."[6] African-Americans suffering from cultural deprivation need a place where they can be taught culture. To right the balance by teaching Blacks their own culture has been a part of Teer's mission since founding the NBT.

In 1968, after Teer had directed Joseph Walker's off-Broadway musical *The Believers*, she was approached by Zuri McKie, a Black opera singer and cast member, who requested that Teer teach her acting. Teer agreed to teach, but only to a group, and she began a workshop at the Martinique Theatre. The class later moved uptown to the Elks Club on a 126th Street and then to the East Wind, a loft that Teer shared with the Last Poets, also in Harlem. Maurice Peterson remembers that

> A doctor donated space for the classes. The Last Poets also donated some space to accommodate the increasing number of her followers. . . . There on 125th Street she and her disciples tried to evolve a new Black art standard.[7]

They worked together for two years. The first year of the theatre's existence was largely experimental: there were no public performances; workshops and symposiums were scheduled each week. Teer has stated that, "First we sacrificed our egos, our desire to act, and went about the task of establishing a black theatrical standard—a standard based on the black lifestyle."[8] The focus of the theatre was determined during the first year of experimentation.

Then in 1969, explains Teer, "Classes at the East Wind loft became too large, although recruitment was only by word of mouth."[9] The NBT was able "to purchase a bare room of 8000 square feet," at 9 East 125th Street, "with help from the people in theatre and from money Teer had received for directing Charlie Russell's *Five on the Black Hand Side* at the American Place Theatre in the same year."[10]

Teer and her group of thirty-five performers sat down and formulated six goals at this time. These included: (1) the creation and perpetuation of a Black art standard, (2) eliminating the competitive aspect of most commercial theatre, (3) re-educating audiences, (4) restoring spirituality and a cultural tradition that Teer felt had been stripped from Blacks in America, (5) creating an alternate system of values to the Western concept, and, (6) creating a Black theory of acting and liberation. I shall now consider each of these goals separately.

GOAL 1: SELF-AFFIRMATION

Teer has stated that "First and foremost was the creation and perpetuation of a Black art standard. A way of working Blackly—so that an artist can work naturally from his own spiritual energies, by using the language, environment, and all elements which distinguished Black people from other nationalities."[11] James Anderson gives a vivid example of one of Teer's distinguishing elements with his comment on language: "The writing/speaking styles of Mexican-American, Black-American, and Puerto Rican-American students are frequently viewed as 'too flowery,' too subjective, involving an excessive use of metaphors, [and] utilizing the wrong tense of verbs."[12] He adds that "What is a valuable and valid communication process under one cognitive style becomes a deformed example of cognitive/linguistic deficits under another."[13] Teer's goal was to have her African-American students find what Anderson calls the "valuable and the valid" by "working Blackly," that is, by studying and working within their own culture. The goal of self-affirmation through the study of one's own culture has also been tested at NBT in unanticipated ways.

An interview with Steve Bustamente, a Colombian member of the graduating class of the Teer Technology of Soul [TTS] in 1992 revealed as much. The student stated that upon arriving in New York he had made friends with African-Americans. His purpose then for coming to TTS was to become better at presenting himself and to learn more about African-Americans. However, the instructors of the TTS first gave Bustamente the task of learning more about Colombia and relating that information to the group. Abisola Faison, one of the TTS instructors, explained that the group wanted to love Bustemente for who he was. At graduation, Bustemente spoke with pride of the information that he had gathered about his native country.

This self-validation, which is the cornerstone of the NBT, was conceived primarily for African-Americans. The basing of the theatre in Harlem, the Black cultural capital of the world, reinforces this fact. Teer contends that knowing and trusting the feelings of Black people was the primary need of Black theatre, and she believes that "You cannot have a theatre without an ideology, without a base from which all of the forms must emanate[,] and call it black, for it will be the same as Western theatre, conventional theatre, safe theatre."[14] From a base in predominantly Black Harlem, Teer was determined to formulate an ideology which departed from the standards in American theatre as they pertained to Black people.

In performance, Teer wanted her students to begin unmasking the feelings and the faces they had disguised in coping with the White world. Woodie King, Jr. explains,

> When an American Negro actor is faced with playing a character, he must confront a trio of problems: First, should the character be American in its truest sense? . . . Second, should he be Negro as Negroes really are or Negro as we have led whites to believe we are in order to endure? And third, should the character be American Negro?[15]

Teer found in King's words a further justification for her goal of self-affirmation.

GOAL 2: COOPERATION

Teer states that "NBT's second major goal was to eliminate the competitive aspect of most commercial theatre. This goal was accomplished through an essential Black medium: the Black family structure."[16] This structure, instilled in Africa, carried over into slavery; for "During slavery," as James Banks points out, "the family was important to the slaves. Family members taught the child how to survive the harsh White environment, as well as how never to submit totally to the whims of the master."[17] Family was important not only to teach survival techniques but to serve as a supportive and collaborative body.

In the NBT, as in many families, there was to be no "star" system; everyone was to be important, but no one was to be indulged. The group became very goal-oriented, not role-oriented; roles were not rigidly defined. Once a goal was established it did not matter who accomplished the task as long as it was completed without complaining. The members of Teer's company were given freedom to experiment; every member was expected to "do everything from sweeping the floors to singing."[18] Accordingly, "sound technicians acted. Actors built sets. Lighting designers danced. Cooperation was Teer's goal; group effort was stressed rather than individual effort."[19] This community spirit which Teer fosters in her theatre company not only develops latent talents in the entire company but also provides a model of the society which she envisions as the ideal result of the NBT's educative efforts: a society based on cooperation rather than on competition.

GOAL 3: EDUCATION

"The third major goal of NBT," writes Jessica Harris, "was to re-educate audiences."[20] Teer stated:

> We need permanent cultural and educational institutions, committed
> to teaching what it means to be human. . . . Art and culture is where
> people are taught values, where substance is produced, where we
> establish traditions and practices and rituals and standards which we
> live our lives by. Culture and art is [sic] where the parameters for
> behaving are developed, how we treat each other, what we hold
> dear.[21]

In commercial theatre financial success has become more important
than teaching values to those who support and participate in it. Teer and
the NBT want to give their community information germane to their
surroundings and to issues which daily confront them. Harris writes
that

> The NBT performances . . . deal with situations that are relevant to
> the members of the Harlem Community. The group attempts and
> usually succeeds in providing the largely Harlem spectators with new
> information about themselves, so that they leave uplifted, reaffirmed,
> and enlightened.[22]

Re-educating has a two-fold purpose: (1) to counteract the damaging
effects of subjugation of African-Americans' minds; and (2) to
cultivate a clear understanding of facts necessary for African-American
survival.

In the NBT production *A Revival,* one actor related information
about how Blacks spend their money to show that although Blacks have
money, they often spend it on seemingly unnecessary material objects:
"We are 11 per cent of the population but we buy 49 per cent of this
country's scotch, spend 8 million dollars on ties and 200 million on
suits and drink 25 per cent of the grape soda."[23] Then he asked the
audience, "How does that relate to positive blackness?"[24]

To expose the greater Harlem area to information about social and
political issues in 1971, Teer instituted Symposiums, later called
Blackenings, on Sunday afternoons. Although these will be discussed
in detail in Chapter Four, Teer stated that a Symposium "is an open
forum where Black people can come and find out directly from the
people involved in cultural-political- [or] economic activities what they

are about."[25] The audience and the Harlem community were thus re-educated about their history, their culture, and their power as consumers.

GOAL 4: SPIRITUALITY

"NBT's fourth goal," writes Harris, "was to restore spirituality and a cultural tradition that Teer felt had been stripped away from Blacks in America."[26] She believed that Black people had been spiritually starved: "The white man's Christianity has so turned us off from religion that we don't believe in anything, not even ourselves," stated Teer, "and we need to believe in ourselves. Each individual needs to get in touch with his natural, organic and spiritual self."[27] After all, she reasoned, Blacks are a spiritual and emotive people:

> We are an African people. And Africans are spirit people. So we must have an ideology that will help us develop a spirit culture. A culture to deal with the spirit. A spirit power, in order to deal with the concept of theatre as a religious experience . . . as a holy experience, as a cleansing experience, as a lifting experience, as a raising experience. As a force or energy to help us transcend ourselves; raise ourselves, so that we can discover the magic in us.[28]

Teer advocated not a dismissal of Christianity or of God but a religion without hypocrisy. She herself had found a spiritual bond with the Yoruba. She stated that embracing African religion is

> not so much a rejection of Christianity as a rejection of what Western Civilization has done to Christianity. Christianity is packaged and presented as a mental thing. . . . there's no experience of the religion. When you go to a Protestant Church there is no emotive power because there is no action, no life force. There is no emotive power allowed to the people. All power is behind the pulpit.[29]

Yet she did find spirituality in Christianity as well as in Yoruba religion. She found it in the Black Pentecostal churches, where freedom of expression was encouraged to a far greater degree than in other churches where, she felt, outward decorum smothered any spiritual sparks.

Once the students at Teer's theatre had kindled their own spirituality, they could then ignite an audience. At performances Teer wanted the participants and the audience to be infused with spirituality, while celebrating being Black and being human.

GOAL 5: VALUES

"Creating an alternative system of values to the Western concept was the fifth goal of NBT,"[30] according to Teer. Through observation and experience Teer and her associates determined that problems of separation resulting in emotional and physical stress were being caused by a breakdown in communication with Africa. Cut off from this source of self-validation, Teer believed, Black Americans had been forced to adopt the standards, values, and lifestyles of Americans with European backgrounds, and this process weakened Blacks. Teer wrote that

> Our technique is all about the strengthening of the mind. We start
> with the premise that the Western system is a very surface system
> opposed to the essence of things, the center, the spirit of people. . . .
> A spiritual journey is the opening of new avenues of thought
> redirecting the concept of who we are and how we must function.[31]

In Teer's view, theatre was a spiritual art form, one that could arise from emotions and awaken them in turn. Some acting teachers and some directors regard strict discipline and conventions as the means by which emotion can be harnessed and safely unleashed. Blacks, Teer felt, are different. She did not want to be confined by strict conventions of blocking, concepts, and styles. She writes:

> My vision of theater is one rooted in the heart, not the mind. I want to
> add another dimension to theatre—the dimension of human spirit, so
> that people will get to experience who they are when they come to
> the theater and not just [look] at the scenery and how pretty the actors

are. It's a billion dollar industry wasted on gimmicks to sell tickets
when in fact the only thing to sell is you—your spirit directly
communicating to somebody else.[32]

The NBT actors do not perform with an invisible fourth wall; they are
as aware of their audience as their audience is of them. Their goal is to
involve every audience spiritually in their performance.

NBT has also sought to develop a "God-conscious" art to replace
European "self-conscious" art which it believed was conditioned by
materialism and based on external feelings. Teer writes that "God-
conscious art is the creative expression coming from within, as opposed
to self-conscious art, which has resulted from European conditioning
and which says that you have to gain external material things to feel
fulfilled."[33]

God-conscious art, according to Teer, is guided by the creative
impulses that emanate from within. She believes it is a way of
performing with spirituality and emotions unleashed, as opposed to
Western traditional standards which, in an effort to sublimate emotional
energy, too often simply represses it.

GOAL 6: LIBERATION

Teer has stated that "The sixth goal of the NBT was to create a Black
theory of acting and liberation."[34] Teer believed that liberation becomes
necessary for Black Americans who, raised in a racist environment,
consider themselves to be second-class citizens. These feelings of
inferiority can hinder the actor in performance, inhibiting that freedom
of expression essential to art. Teer urges NBT members to make
themselves responsible for their state of mind regardless of what
happens to them. This sense of responsibility, she feels, liberates them
from the negative forces of society, enabling them to become
autonomous creators and liberators.

Harris writes that

As the Black experience in America is quite different from the White
one, Black actors are frequently asked to play roles that have nothing

to do with the basic reality of their lives. This may seem to be a
contradiction but Stanislavski's "as if" theory does not always work
for Black actors in these times. With the theories established by the
NBT, the Black actor can return to himself, to his culture, to his
heritage, and to his people.[35]

Stanislavski's "magic if" treats "if" as a word which "can transform our
thoughts. . . . Through it we can imagine ourselves in virtually every
situation."[36] This particular doctrine becomes destructive for many
African-Americans, whom "if" can make very angry. "If there had not
been slavery," "If I was White," "If there was no racism," "If I could
get a good job" are hypotheses African-Americans must often use,
defeating the purpose of Stanislavski's exercise and providing a
negative force with which to reckon before the real work can begin.
Instead of inviting the actor to forget himself and step into another soul,
the NBT immerses him in self-study, not only of who he is but of his
roots. Teer has remarked that

> If you really want to know about a people look at their beliefs. Their
> Gods. Before history books got turned all around you could tell
> people by what they believed in . . . not by the history [,] the set of
> facts selected and put down according to some individual's ordered
> mind.[37]

In order to help herself understand her Black roots, Teer applied
for and received a Ford Foundation Fellowship in 1972 to visit seven
African countries to research "soul" through African ancestry. She
spent four months in Western Nigeria acquainting herself fully with the
Yoruba culture and religion. Teer stated that she "was supposed to visit
seven countries in Africa and spend a couple of weeks in each, but
ended up spending all the time in Oshogbo, a small village in Nigeria
where she was initiated into the Yoruba religion as a Yoruba priestess.
Her students in 1969 gave her the new name of, Roho Taji Taifu, which
means 'Spirit of the Royal Nation.'"[38]

Teer returned to Nigeria seven times between 1972 and 1974. She
and her performing company of thirty-five students continued their

research into other parts of the Black world: Africa, South America, the West Indies, Guyana, Haiti, and Trinidad.

In Nigeria, Teer and her group became acquainted with a male Nigerian artist, Twin Seven-Seven, as they tried to "build a cultural base between the cultural expressions of Africans and African Americans in Harlem."[39] Teer states that the "whole affair is sort of cross-fertilization. Black theatre provides English as the medium of its expression: the Twin Seven-Seven teaches his Afro-American colleagues Yoruba."[40] He and Teer's group lived together and performed together for three months in Oshogbo, Nigeria, the home of the Twin Seven-Seven, in preparation for a performance at FESTAC, the 2nd World Festival of Black and African Arts and culture in Lagos. Teer also brought the Twin Seven-Seven to Harlem to perform, and his association with NBT remains close. Meanwhile, Teer and her actors continue to travel regularly to Africa.

THE NBT'S PERFORMANCE GOALS

After Teer had set goals for the NBT, she and her members initiated goals for their productions. They had very definite ideas of what theatre should do in order to liberate. Teer stated:

> Our art standard requires that all theatrical presentations, be they dramatic plays, musicals, rituals, or revivals must:

1. RAISE THE LEVEL OF CONSCIOUSNESS through liberating the spirits and strengthening the minds of its people.
2. BE POLITICAL, that is it must deal in a positive manner with the existing conditions of oppression.
3. In some ways EDUCATE and educate to bring out that which is already within and give knowledge and truth.
4. CLARIFY ISSUES, that is enlighten the participants as to why so many negative conditions and images exist in their community in order to eliminate the negative condition and strengthen the positive condition.
5. Lastly, it must ENTERTAIN.[41]

Teer felt that the key to attaining these objectives was to discover the science and the secret of "soul." The seventh definition of "soul" in *Webster's Third New International Pocket Dictionary* describes it "as a strong, positive feeling (as of intense sensitivity and emotional fervor) conveyed esp. by American Negro performers . . . of, relating to, or characteristic of American Negroes or their culture, . . . designed for or controlled by Negroes."[42] Teer's own views on the matter are fully consistent with this definition, and her own notion of "soul" is represented in her statement that

> Singing, dancing those are the things that take you down. When we sing and it gets so good we go down. The singers in the Gospel choirs dip their knees and get down, we go down and into ourselves. For the power. To touch the forces. And when they are touched, when it gets so good we release the power in a scream. You know. That's power. That's emotion. That is feeling, primal, unrefined feeling is force. . . . And when you go into the Holly [*sic*] Roller church, the Pentecostal churches and when you see African Religious festivals . . . Bimbes, or when you see Haitian ceremonies. People are moving. They're dancing. They're praising. They're singing. It goes on and on. You know, they are drumming. They're stomping . . . and they're down . . . and they release this spirit and they get power. They kiss the Earth when they give praise. They don't look up to the sky. They go down to the ground where it is practical.[43]

Teer believes that "soul" people are a practical people whose element is Earth. Teer also believes that "soul" is not only a force but a feeling. She describes particular sounds which make up the feeling of soul:

> When you go down 125th Street or in any Black community you hear music all the time and it's blasting . . . out to the suburbs it's clean, clean, clean and quiet, quiet, quiet. . . . When you go into the Black community people live side by side. In the south, in Harlem and not always for force of ghettoization. Rather by force of feeling.[44]

"Soul" brothers and sisters represented to Teer those who could identify with the discrimination that Blacks had encountered in

America. When racism damages a person, Teer believes, it goes to the very core of that person's being, to his very soul: he is rejected not for a mere "offense," he is rejected for what he is. Although Whites and others can sympathize, Teer feels, they cannot fully understand the impact of such a blow unless they are kindred souls. Ultimately, Teer stated, "soul" "is the awesome gift, a cultural phenomenon that swells up inside where the spirit resides. It can be present when a person is in touch with the divine energy of God."[45]

"Soul," then, is the key to Teer's acting method; and to put audiences in touch with "soul" is the purpose of her theatre, for soul is the essence of spirituality. As Harris writes, "The National Black Theatre does not consider entertainment its overriding goal. Its major goal is to re-educate, to restore spirituality and a cultural tradition that Teer believes has been stripped from blacks in America."[46] Art can serve this educative function, according to Teer, because it reflects the culture that produced it. But for this very reason, according to Teer, it is important to choose carefully the sources from which to create an art that is to educate a people: "Black life-style must be the source of artistic expression if there is to be a Black Theatre for a Black Nation."[47] For Teer the foundations of this cultural institution lay in training artists, theatrically and spiritually, in the spirit of an African-American lifestyle.

NOTES

1. Linda James Myers, "The Nature of Pluralism and the African American Case, *Theory into Practice*," vol. 20, (1981), 3.

2. Myers, 5.

3. James Anderson, "Cognitive Styles and Multicultural Populations," *Journal of Teacher Education* (Jan.-Feb., 1988), 7.

4. Anderson, 4.

5. Myers, 5.

6. "The Issue is Race," mod. Phil Donahue, *MacNeil/Lehrer News Hour* PBS, WNET, New York, 15 Sept. 1992, 473.

7. Maurice Peterson, "Spotlight on Barbara Ann Teer," *Essence* (Aug., 1975), 19.

8. Charlie L. Russell, "Barbara Ann Teer: We Are Liberators Not Actors, " *Essence* (March, 1971), 48-49.

9. "Barbara Ann Teer and The National Black Theatre," *Interreligious Foundation for Community Organization News*. Jan.-Feb., 1972, 1.

10. *Interreligious Foundation for Community Organization News*, 1.

11. The six goals listed are all taken from a pamphlet entitled "NBT Is a Celebration of Life AND A REBIRTH OF POWER" (New York: n.p., 1973), 6. Each of the goals will be classified as "REBIRTH OF POWER."

12. Anderson, 7.

13. Anderson, 7.

14. Jessica B. Harris, "The National Black Theatre: The Sun People of 125th Street," in *The Theatre of Black Americans* (New York: Applause, 1987), 283.

15. Woodie King, Jr., "Problems Facing Negro Actors," *The International Library of Negro Life and History Anthology of the American Negro in the Theatre*, 2nd ed., ed. Lindsay Patterson (New York: Publishers Company, Inc., 1969),141.

16. "REBIRTH OF POWER," 6.

17. James A. Banks, *Teaching Strategies for Ethnic Studies*, 5th ed. (Boston: Allyn and Bacon, 1991), p. 198.

18. Ruth Husar, "She Celebrates the Black Life-Style," *Bridgeport Post*, 9 August 1974, Bridgeport, Connecticut, n. pag.

19. Harris, 284-285.

20. "REBIRTH OF POWER," 6.

21. "The Issue is Race," 457, 461.

22. Harris, 285.

23. Clarence Allsopp, "The National Black Theatre Gets Set to Revive Harlem," *NY Amsterdam News*, 22 July 1972, D-3.

24. Allsopp, D-3.

25. Martha M. Jones, "Barbara Ann Teer's National Black Theatre," *Black Creation* vol. 3, no. 4 (Summer 1972), 20.

26. "REBIRTH OF POWER," 6.

27. Russell, 50.

28. Russell, 50.

29. Charles Burden, "A Trip to Africa Brings Hope to America," *Newsworld* 2 June 1980, 2B.

30. "REBIRTH OF POWER," 6.

31. Quoted in Thomas A. Johnson, "On Harlem Stage, A Spiritual Journey," *New York Times*, 11 May 1971, E-44.

32. Burden, 1.

33. "Barbara Ann Teer: Producer," *Ebony*, vol. 32, no. 10, (August 1977),138.

34. "REBIRTH OF POWER," 6.

35. Harris, 285.

36. Edwin Wilson, *The Theater Experience*, 5th ed. (New York: McGraw-Hill Publishing Co., 1991), p. 104.

37. Quoted in Curtiss E. Porter, "THIS HERE CHILD IS NAKED AND FREE AS A BIRD: AN ANNOTATED INTERVIEW WITH BARBARA ANN TEER," *Black Lines*, vol. 2, No. 3 (spring 1973), 40. Because this article was transcribed from an oral presentation there are many errors in punctuation and grammar. What is important is that the essence of Teer's message is evident. Herein will be listed as Teer interview by Porter.

38. Husar, 1.

39. Kawe, "International Cooperation in Drama," *Sunday Sketch*, 9 September 1973, 1. Twin Seven-Seven refers to a musician who is one of the seventh set of twins in his family. In Africa, twins are considered sacred: spiritually and creatively blessed. Twin Seven-Seven was an actor, a musician, a dancer, and an intuitive and spontaneous performer.

40. Kawe, 1.

41. Harris, 283-284.

42. *The Merriam-Webster Dictionary* (New York: Pocket Books, 1974), p. 657.

43. Teer interview by Porter, 25.

44. Teer interview by Porter, 25- 26.

45. Barbara Ann Teer, "The National Black Institute of Action Arts," Part of advertising pamphlet for *The Legacy* Tour USA 1989, 3.

46. Harris, 285.

47.Husar,1.

The official National Black Theatre Logo adopted in 1969 and designed by George Ford. The logo is called "MAX" and represents the maximum spirit inherent in people of African descent.

Dr. Barbara Ann Teer and the National Black Theatre at their 10th Anniversary Celebration with a Performance of *Soljourney into Truth* at the Beacon Theatre in New York on Broadway and 74th Street, May 1979.

Dr. Barbara Ann Teer, director, playwright, and performer, *Soljourney into Truth*, May 1979.

The National Black Theatre's building on 125th Street at Fifth Avenue after the catastrophic fire in March of 1983.

Front entrance of the National Black Theatre's Institute of Action
Arts complex built in 1990. Photo by Jim Belfon.

Northeast corner of the National Black Theatre's Institute of Action Arts at 125th Street and Fifth Avenue. Photo by Jim Belfon.

Newly renamed streets in front of the National Black Theatre's Institute of Action Arts, signed into law by the mayor of New York on May 31, 1994. Local laws Number 10 and 11 changed 125th Street to Frederica Boulevard and Fifth Avenue to National Black Theatre Way. Photo by Jim Belfon.

IV

Training at the National Black Theatre

Stepping into nothingness thru language I come
Inventing my own reality thru language I come
Bathing in I Amness thru language I come
I mean . . .
I can fly like a bird in the sky I Am that I Am!

Barbara Ann Teer, "Living in the Lite," 1991

The foundation of the National Black Theatre lies in its classes and workshops. Its productions have been supported by the study and participation required of the performers in the NBT classes. It has been important to Teer to have not only a theatre company with a new ideology, but also a process by which artists could be trained to apply her theories of performance.

This chapter will begin by focusing on the original classes Teer and her actors formulated. Then it will describe the current classes offered. I will examine the goals and processes of each class and its connection to the overriding philosophy of the theatre. I will develop such connections in the light of Teer's writings, personal interviews with her, her students, and graduates, and my observations of various classes between 1987 and 1992. Finally, I will consider a graduation ceremony which brings together the basic elements of Teer's approach.

For a prospective student at the NBT, as with many theatre training programs, becoming a student begins with an application form; however the NBT also requires a commitment form. This form is actually a contract, stipulating that the applicant who signs it will have good attendance, be punctual, come to class prepared, and fully participate in all activities throughout the course.

Beginning in 1969, Teer began to organize experimental classes based upon her theories of performance. During this time Teer and her students investigated various theatrical methods. They constantly evaluated, modified, and devised new courses. By the mid-1970s, courses were offered in evolutionary movement and dance, meditation, spiritual release, numerology, astrology, liberation theory and practice, and ideology. The subject matter of each class follows with definitions, process, and results.

EVOLUTIONARY MOVEMENT AND DANCE COURSE

Teer herself conducted an Evolutionary Movement and Dance class, to teach participants about their African roots through information and physical movement. She covered the geography, resources, people, and demographics of Africa, with attention to the drums used for communication and recreation. In addition, she compared the African drum music to popular rhythm-and-blues and all forms of "soul" music. She even asked students to stand and move to the beat of the music to African drum pieces and to varied rhythms from popular Black American, West Indian, and South American recording artists.

Teer played recorded music as she began speaking to the group, and she spoke poetry and guiding phrases, as students moved about the room to the beat of the music. Often, Teer asked students to show specified emotions and characteristics through body movements, and there evolved from such exercises dances representing love, pride, joy, and ecstasy. The class sessions, lasting between one-half and one hour, were followed by the participants discussing what they had felt and why they had moved as they did. Afterward they watched a film of the NBT's trip to Africa, and they compared their movements to those of the Yoruba Tribe as captured in the film.

Many students found that their movements resembled movements used by the African people, and so they often attributed the pattern of their movements to their African ancestry. According to Teer,

> The Evolutionary Movement was designed for the student to experience his body as a "cosmic miracle," so that his self-consciousness would dissolve. Through this experience the student would begin to know more about his body and thereby be more exuberantly alive.[1]

Teer believed that the "cosmic miracle" would dispel the myth that Blacks were rendered ugly by their skin tone, hair texture, or facial features. She felt that by throwing off the physical as well as psychological limitations imposed by such stereotypes, the students might celebrate the marvel of their bodies coming from an act of God.

Teer also helped students who had problems with physical coordination, taking time to work with them individually. Her extensive dance experience with Mary Wigman and Etienne Decroux enabled her to suggest exercises, improvisations, and other instructors who could help further. Teer also was aided by dance and movement teachers including Charles Moore, Eleo Pomare, Silvia Waters, Rod Rogers, and Pearl Primus.[2] Primus is typical of this group in contending that "dancing is a means of communicating to others . . . deep emotional and intellectual feelings about democracy and about the Negro as a race and as a member of the society in which he lives."[3]

The Evolutionary Movement class also provided an opportunity for students to begin to admire their own bodies. One exercise required the students to gaze each day at their reflections, first in a hand-held mirror and then in a full-length mirror, in order to see and know their bodies better. Students were also sent to libraries to obtain anatomical information about the body, as another way to understand more about each part of themselves.

MEDITATION AND SPIRITUAL RELEASE COURSES

The Evolutionary Movement Class ran concurrently with classes in Meditation and Spiritual Release, because Teer was interested in having the students work on their bodies, minds, and spirits simultaneously. Classes in meditation, spiritual release, numerology, and astrology were led by Neferlyn Gray, a Harlem clairvoyant and expert on tarot and the occult. In addition, social workers, psychiatrists, and performing and visual artists were called in at various times for workshops, testifying to Teer's aim of cultivating her students' creativity by exposing them to various experiences. Teer stated that the NBT studies the occult sciences "because we want to find out more about our innate abilities. . . . We are concerned with the universal laws: what they are, how they function. We have set up our structure, based on the structure of nature, the universe."[4]

The NBT classes also investigated the order of the United States in relation to the Western hemisphere; this hemisphere in relation to the planet; and the planet in relation to the universe—all of these in order to determine the students' own relation to the whole. Teer's plan, then, was to aid each student in discovering his own importance, his specific purpose for existing, and in helping to dispel any feelings of unworthiness. The Spiritual Release and Meditation classes were occasions for students to learn the importance of having time for themselves—time to meditate and get in touch with their feelings and to assess their attributes. They learned the importance of being in harmony with heart, mind, and body, and of striking a balance between their mental, physical, and spiritual beings. In addition to exploring spiritual matters, they were encouraged to become more health-conscious and to begin eating more wholesome foods, and to exercise to keep their bodies healthy. Teer also taught the importance of fasting for purifying the body and disciplining the mind. She noted that

> Fasting is the method we employ to clean the mind as well as the body, a discipline to aid concentration. . . . Fasting can be likened to a house cleaning; you feel better about a clean house. . . . fasting is a spiritual experience as well as a healthful one.[5]

Teer felt that fasting would aid the concentration and discipline her students needed to keep up with the challenges that she had set for them.

When Teer was criticized for her emphasis on mythology and the occult sciences courses, she responded that "By studying the occult sciences they are in search of the structure and function of universal laws. Anyway, I know I'm not a witch. I'm just a normal Black woman who wants to do something for Black people."[6] Teer was interested in knowledge for herself and her students. To Teer, knowledge was the best weapon against feelings of low self-esteem. Therefore, Teer advocated that her students have strong bodies and healthy minds filled with knowledge.

LIBERATION THEORY CLASSES

Classes in Liberation Theory and Practice were called "The Master Liberation Workshop" and the "Pyramid Processes One" and "Two." The Master Liberation Workshop was a seven-hour course designed by Teer to demonstrate to the student that he is responsible for everything in his own life. Despite the title "workshop," the courses consisted principally of lectures by Teer on the positive values of America and Americans and of Africa and Africans. Teer also had students take deep breaths, breathing in the "positive" and expelling the "negative" so as to change how they walked, talked, and felt about their lives. She had her students assume the deportment of African princes and the voice and bearing of giants. The Master Liberation Workshop, according to Teer, was "designed to put 'you' in touch with 'your' power so that you could transform your life and increase 'your' ability to attract and hold more prosperity, aliveness, happiness and joy."[7]

After the workshop, Teer believed, students would better understand that they could control their own lives and that they did not have to be underprivileged or culturally deprived. They could remain victims or, with help, they could choose to recast their lives. According to Teer, any individual can "come from perfection and behold himself as a perfect human being and move from that space."[8] The workshop helped participants to break out of their shells, which Teer believed to be self-imposed. In 1975, Teer explained how the goals of the Master Liberation Workshop were achieved:

> In order to realize total liberation, this workshop moves participants towards an inward cleansing of the mind. Through a comparative analysis of two different evolutionary systems, one African and one European, participants get to choose a point of view about life which assists them in removing the notion that Black people are oppressed, and helps them get more satisfaction out of life.[9]

The second and third steps of Liberation Theory were the Pyramid Processes One and Two, both of them eight-week courses. Teer stated that their purpose was "to enable the participants to present themselves fearlessly to the world and to enjoy that presentation of who they were."[10] Power, according to Teer, "was the ability to take action."[11] This power was aimed not at securing wealth or political influence, but at dispelling fear, inferiority, and naiveté so that the students might walk down any street and look anyone directly in the eye. Teer sought to inspire her students to feel positive about all things. If, for example, they were prevented by illness from attending some special event, they were not to be depressed but rather to understand that they were just not meant to be there. If their financial situation was regrettable, they were urged to inventory their resources and to apply for a higher-paying job.

"The Pyramid Process of Performing Class," according to Teer, "was designed to discover and expand . . . natural/creative power that swells spontaneously from within."[12] Each student would be able, according to Teer, to "rediscover and master that magnetic entity called soul and express himself in a whole new way so that he can perform effortlessly and without fear."[13] Teer assured each student that he could become an accomplished person if he believed in himself.

The Pyramid Process Two course, also called the "Ritualization of Communication," was for more advanced students. "Its purpose," according to Teer, "was to further remove concepts of lack, limitation, and self-consciousness."[14] To free themselves of feelings of inadequacy, the students performed continuously either before an audience or before the class. Teer encouraged them at every opportunity, in novel and sometimes surprising ways. For example, she wrote a musical for Zuri McKie, a student interested in opera performance. Teer reported that, "Zuri wanted to sing again and I supported her. What I had to do was write a piece that would present her in a fashion that she'd be comfortable with. . . . I wrote it [*Softly Comes a Whirlwind*] for her out of my love for her."[15]

Three other exercises helped prospective performers to understand and achieve the goals of liberation theory. The first exercise engaged the participant in a "love affair" with himself. Teer's theory was that by loving oneself, one can become self-motivated, love others, and educate others through love. Students had to write out all the good deeds they had done in their lives, no matter how small. These deeds could be as minute as sharing a meal or clothing, or as great as saving a person's life.

The students also began each class by hugging themselves and hugging every other person in the class, and then, before they were seated, they were to hug themselves again. Next, they took out mirrors and kissed themselves, and while looking in the mirrors they repeated, "Hello, beautiful, you are Somebody." This exercise was not intended as an exercise in narcissism, but rather to exorcise the painful results of racism and prejudice.

Some of the students' feelings of unworthiness arose out of actual experiences such as being called a "nigger," being turned away from a restaurant, or being denied a job. Others were self-imposed, the results of a long series of historical and social injustices, including indoctrination in school, where historical facts about Blacks were either distorted or ignored and where unflattering stereotypes were perpetuated. Teer believed that students without self-esteem could not act for her or for others, and that such esteem could develop only after negative feelings had been removed. She believed that self-esteem lowered the barriers of embarrassment and inhibition and widened the range of characters the students felt free to explore.

The second exercise, named the "de-crudding" process, was designed to eradicate feelings of worthlessness and self-contempt. The "de-crudding" process identified the worth in a person and helped him appreciate and love himself. Teer explained that the "de-crudding" process was a "purification process undertaken by the prospective actors to find whatever was at their base as individuals."[16] For many students there remained, for instance, some disgrace attached to living in Harlem. Harlemites were often considered dangerous persons, criminals, or security risks. The "de-crudding" process was an opportunity for participants to "soul search for their identity and positive attributes, and to understand that they could rise above the negative associations attaching them to their community. Teer believed that the process helped students discover their roots, learn what being "Black" meant, and understand that there was pride in being an African-American. Most of the process involved furnishing information about Blacks, especially about their accomplishments dating back to Cleopatra and Nefertiti. Many Blacks had not received this information in school, and many had been taught, for instance, that Cleopatra was White, and had seen this misconception confirmed on television and in films.

One activity that illustrates the "de-crudding" process required a student to stand in the center of a room surrounded by seated students. Each seated student would shout out an insult, such as "You're as ugly as a dog," or "You're stupid." The standing student would have to refute each insult with a defense based on logic, such as "I am not ugly. I am a human being made in the image of God. God is beauty; therefore, I am beauty," or "I am not ignorant. I am a learned individual. Much of my education has involved misrepresentation of the truth but I am embracing true knowledge; ignorant people do not embrace true knowledge; therefore, I am not ignorant." This exercise encouraged students to speak out about themselves, so that they would not believe racial slurs and would have verbal weapons to defend their merits.

BLACK CULTURAL RESOURCES: PENTECOSTAL CHURCH

Another exercise which was part of the Liberation class were visits to a highly emotional Pentecostal church and a lively bar, both in the center of Harlem, on the assumption that in such surroundings people show most clearly who they are. In such surroundings, Teer believed, students could gain further insight into the character of their own people.

During their visits, the students encountered people from all classes and walks of life. The observations made at the church and at the bar had a two-fold purpose: (1) to see Black people from varied professions; and (2) to see those people reacting to a relaxed setting. Teer has explained that

> We set out to establish a theatrical concept based on the Black life-style and we borrowed heavily from the churches. . . . We went into the churches, not the Episcopal churches, but the Pentecostal churches, the Baptist churches, . . . where blackness was most clearly expressed. For us blackness is a spiritual value. . . . We measured that value based on how free people were—Black people are really free in church.[17]

This "free spirit" technique was an emotional and spiritual experience involving students' observations of body movements stimulated by the feelings and thoughts. Teer wanted her students to discover the close connection between the spirit and the senses. This is partly why she included church attendance in her curriculum, and continues to do so. During the church services that Teer's students attend, members of the congregation and visitors are often encouraged to express their love, joy, happiness, sadness vocally or physically and without embarrassment. As I pointed out in Chapter Two, it is not uncommon to see members, during any part of the worship service, scream, cry, and wave their arms. Members of the congregation eagerly clap their hands, tap their feet, shake their heads, and sway their bodies as they begin to feel the spirit. This does not distract attention from the service, but rather fuels the fire which has been generated by the minister's prayer or by a song from the choir.

An onlooker at these proceedings might believe that the members are crazy or fanatic—or even that they are faking such experiences. However, to the members themselves, these experiences are very important. The worshipers are simply obeying scripture: "Make a joyful noise unto the Lord, all ye lands. Serve the Lord with gladness and come before his presence with singing."[18] Occasionally, a member will begin a holy dance, some running all about the church, and some running to the altar and remaining there until they felt blessed by God. Many times this experience results in crying, sometimes in rolling on the floor in humility, and sometimes in foaming at the mouth for purification. Teer's students often find themselves caught up in these services.

The physical warm-up exercises in many university acting classes closely resemble these experiences at Pentecostal churches. Students are taught to move with feeling. The physical warm-up known as "shake everything out," for instance, requires students to expel their tension through breathing, to release it with a sigh or a physical movement. After an effective acting class or stage performance, many students find themselves exhausted but fulfilled, much as worshippers feel after a church service during which the spirit has been manifested. Thorough interaction—whether with fellow actors or with God—taxes the body to reward the spirit, and this is the sort of energy Teer sought to evoke by taking her students to churches.

The climax of the Pentecostal church service is usually the minister's sermon, which is both emotional and dramatic. During the sermon, a Pentecostal minister might strike the pulpit or even jump on top of it. Nor does he remain in the pulpit or rostrum area, but he might take a microphone and go down into the congregation. He might also establish a rhythm, keeping the beat by tapping his foot or clapping his hands. His sermon is in many ways a theatrical enactment of his biblical text. Such rhythmic preaching descends from its roots in Africa, in rhythms used by the griot or storyteller. Teer surmised that it was essentially a Black idiom and so wanted to instill it in her students.

After they had attended church services, Teer asked her students to practice facial and body movements, striving to re-enact the feelings they had experienced at the church. They use not only biblical stories but fairy tales and daily events from their lives to perform before the class in a "preacher-rhythm." Standing within a circle of classmates who become his congregation, each participant then performs his own story. Just as interaction from the congregation is essential to the church services and the minister's sermon, this same interchange takes place in the NBT's classes. Furthermore, the NBT productions always include interaction with the audiences, so students learn how to accomplish this task first by observation, then by simulation, and then by actual performing.

In addition to experiencing church services, Teer and her group sought out the ministers, deacons, and women of the church, to question them about the service. Teer has said that "We asked them all sorts of questions. Religious questions. How they organized things? Why they wore white? About how they get possessed and speak in tongues? How they got people to come to church every Sunday?"[19] On the basis of the answers she received, Teer was able to conclude that "There are many concrete reasons why the church is our oldest and strongest institution. . . . [M]any of our basic techniques come directly from the Black Church."[20] The Pentecostal church service, which was the only service the NBT classes attended for this exercise, was a necessary element of Teer's training because she was advocating a "move from a self-conscious art to a God-conscious art," in order to "discover a whole new way of fully expressing the actor."[21]

The visits to churches are an important part of Teer's curriculum. They also provide therapy for actors engaged in Black "domestic drama." The term domestic drama was coined by White critics who categorized the many Black dramas written on the Black family, such as *A Raisin in the Sun*, *Ceremonies in Dark Old Men*, and *Who's Got His Own*. Teer's criticism of this drama was aimed at the three-part structure and its printed script. Directors were careful that the actors said their lines *verbatim* and stayed faithful to the playwright's intent. Teer, then, felt inclined

> to resent Black domestic drama because that type of form suppresses or compresses the energy. You're not free to be spontaneous and to let go because the form is more important than the feeling. So what I wanted to do is transcend the form and channel the feeling into the experience of who we are. It's difficult to come from your experience and NOT from your feelings, which are illusionary anyway—they go up, and they go down—so the technique I developed, Pyramid Process of Performing, trains people to be fearless on stage and to enjoy themselves being spontaneous and natural.[22]

Teer was also not interested in performing dramas where Blacks struggled with a problem of racism. Instead, she was interested in performances which celebrated the culture of African-Americans. As an example, she used the services at Pentecostal churches which, rather than showing how horrible it was to be a sinner, celebrated how wonderful it was to be God's child. Although Teer and her students attended some unorthodox Baptist churches which believed in shouting and other charismatic characteristics, she was more inclined towards the Pentecostal churches where she and her students felt the services were more related to their interests in the theatre.

BLACK CULTURAL RESOURCES: THE APOLLO THEATRE

Teer often took students on expeditions to the Apollo Theatre in Harlem. She has stated that

> Our most significant learning experiences about black people came from the Apollo Theatre. We went to the Apollo so often they started letting us in free. We studied the different performers, and we began to understand how they related to an audience. We began to discover how they did what they did to the audience.[23]

The atmosphere at the Apollo is, in many ways, similar to that fostered by religious services. Performers are given freedom to experiment, and the audiences are free with their responses. Audiences disapprove boisterously when they dislike a performance and clap enthusiastically when they like one. Teer and her group were able to see performances and to observe reactions by the audience. They then looked for ways to incorporate this spirit and energy into their own work.

THE CYCLES

The healing process, according to Teer, is long and arduous, involving five stages which she calls cycles: "From observations made in [the church, the Apollo Theatre and the bar] the participant can begin to build his own interpretations of the Five Cycles of Evolution, which are at the base of the technique for the NBT actor."[24] Teer's terminology for the five cycles originated from the rhetoric of the 1960s and early 1970s; i.e., Black power, militancy, civil rights, and revolution. This now-dated rhetoric need not, however, obscure Teer's basic categories:

First, THE NIGGER. The Nigger is the most free, most colorful and most creative character. But he has strong materialistic and individualistic values.

Second, THE NEGRO. The Negro is also individualistic and materialistic. He accepts white cultural standards and is an imitation of a White American imitating Europeans, imitating Romans, imitating Greeks, who we all know were imitating Africans.

Third, THE MILITANT. The Militant is an aware Nigger, still individualistic and materialistic. He's in that I-hate-all-White-people bag but he's not for real change, and is only angry and frustrated because the system won't let him in.

Fourth, THE NATIONALIST. The Nationalist is non-materialistic. He is intellectually for the collective. This is the first step into true blackness, where you develop a consciousness and a love for your people. And

Fifth, THE REVOLUTIONARY. The cycle of the revolutionary is the highest, the most evolved of all the cycles, for in this cycle you deal with the spirituality of blackness. You know who you are, what you have to do and you simply go about quietly doing it.[25]

These cycles represented Teer's sense of the internal changes necessary before external ones could take place. The characters of the cycles, representative of the people of Harlem, could move either up or down the vertical scale.[26] Teer understood the cycles as representations of qualities in Black life. An actor, she believed, found the salient characteristics of each cycle and used them for his work on a character. The cycles were not restrictive; they were merely guidelines and thus offered an open arena in which an actor could work. Teer admitted: "Of course you can't put real people in such categories. . . . In real life all of us [Blacks] have the same tendencies; it's just a matter of emphasis. But as a technique it [The Five Cycles] is a good guideline, a basis for a Black theatrical standard."[27] When analyzing the five character types in Teer's classroom, students are encouraged to deal with each in terms of color, music, values, and other indications of Black lifestyle.

According to Teer, The Nigger was colorful, bold, and flamboyant. Bright reds, yellows, and oranges adorned his body. Energized and high spirited, he did not know any other way to gain attention. He felt inferior because of the color of his skin, or possibly because he was not educated, and he felt that the bright colors of his clothing would give him status.

The Negro, according to Teer, is the opposite extreme of a "Nigga" and wanted approval and acceptance from Anglo-Saxon Protestant culture. His existence as an African was hindered by his wishful acceptance of White ideals. His imitations faded his blackness, figuratively speaking, to gray. And indeed, a Black represented by this type of ideology is labeled by some young Blacks as "Gray-Boy" or "Gray-Girl" - Integrationist.

The Militant, according to Teer, was enraged underneath a haze of white lace or metallic gold yarn, indicating that inside he wanted to be accepted but reform was the solution to change the injustices of the system. He wanted to change positions and felt guilty because he knew that he was wrong. His frustration was seen in the anger of the black, brown, and white spots of the leopard; he continually changed places with Whites. Therein was the cause of his anger against the system.

The Nationalist was cynically resigned and had lost interest in material things, according to Teer. He had no desire to prove to whites that black is beautiful. His color was tan, for although he took a stand he was still unsure of himself and wished to remain bland. He was a separatist.

Teer believed that the Revolutionary did not ask, beg, or desire acceptance or approval. He presented himself to the world fearlessly and defiantly by saying it could accept him or reject him. His color was green to signify not only the growth that he had attained, but the development he had reached in caring more about what he thought of himself than about what others thought of him.

At the end of each class Teer encouraged her students, as a final project, to create workbooks using magazine and newspaper clippings, song titles and lyrics, and swatches of material to illustrate each of the five cycles. These workbooks were meant to illustrate that the cycles were constantly changing.

COMMUNITY INVOLVEMENT

At the close of the workshops there was a graduation ceremony for the participants, whom Teer believed ready to begin community service. According to Teer,

> Community service is the next step in their training and development. Everyone goes through two semesters of classes, followed by community work in prisons, [or] hospitals. After that stage, they are ready for membership. Of course, that's when the work really begins.[28]

An example of some of the community services that the NBT provided were rummage sales at least twice a year to sell clothing, furniture, and appliances at very low prices to the people in Harlem. If residents stated that they needed something and did not have the money, Teer would give it to them free of charge. This was part of Teer's belief in showing love to all Blacks. Her students, likewise, were not only to love the community during a performance, but to continue that love after the performance was over.

As another community service project, the NBT began a full-time day care center, open for at least twelve hours a day. This center provided a service for Harlem residents, as well as an opportunity to train the young people who attended the day care in theatre. The center also afforded an opportunity of teaching children in Harlem about theatre.[29]

Another part of the training at the NBT involved Sunday symposiums. These were designed by Teer

> to bring the "Black Community" together in a harmonious atmosphere, to dig on [experience, question, and talk to] cultural performers, and to hear Black scholars, educators, religious people, and community groups of different persuasions . . . express their views and opinions and insights, and to exchange information and visions on specific subjects. . . . This aspect of NBT is designed to fill a vacuum left by the media that *do* not accurately write stories concerning the Black community.[30]

Harlemites were invited to spend the day at the NBT and enjoy a guest speaker, a question-and-answer period, and, if time permitted, a performance of theatre or of dance. The symposiums, called "The Blackening Program," were described by Tony Best as "the product of the Theatre group's search for a theatrical form to house the overwhelming force called Blackness."[31]

These symposiums, according to Best, covered diverse topics:

> James Foreman talked about his rationale for walking into the white churches. . . . Stokely Carmichael spoke about Africans and Afro-Americans alike; Biafrans talked about the "Nigerian War"; the "Gangs" talked about their ideology; Alice Coltrane talked about what motivates her music; Imamu Amiri Baraka discussed his political views; Don L. Lee related the purpose and content of his poetry; welfare mothers related the reality of their lives. There has also been a whole series of programs on drug addiction. NBT Symposiums have dealt with almost every type of situation that exists in the Black community.[32]

Speakers also included Nikki Giovanni, Ruby Dee, Sonia Sanchez, Michael Olatunji, Rod Rogers, Arthur Mitchell, Judge Bruce Wright, Dr. Josef ben Jochannon, H. Rap Brown, and Maya Angelou.[33] African-American artifacts have also been on display, and books and other consciousness-raising materials have been set out for viewing.

The Blackenings opened and closed with meditation.[34] Teer stated that her aim was "to close the space and thank God and ourselves for being loving and harmonious. People can stay around and eat. We have a restaurant where we can eat, socialize some more, hang out, dance and generally have a good time."[35] On occasion, the Blackenings also included White speakers, for Teer's view was that Whites are a part of Blacks' lives. Her theatre was not one of militancy, and the revolution it sought to bring about was not social but spiritual, taking place in the hearts and minds of Blacks. The Blackenings thus offered another opportunity for Teer's students and the citizens of Harlem to be entertained, enlightened, and educated.

CURRENT CLASSES

Graduation from one class usually led to enrollment in other NBT classes. In 1975, Teer and her group re-evaluated the classes, continuing those which were thought most necessary, modifying others, and creating new ones to meet the needs of the students. Enrollment had grown larger, and it was necessary to enlarge the curriculum to accommodate students who wanted to continue working with Teer. Among the courses added were the "Teer Technology of Soul" [TTS] One and Two, which are the principal performance classes meeting twice a week for two months. Classes in "Identity, Dignity and Trust" and "Advanced Public Performance" are subsidiaries and are scheduled for participants who want more training. The sessions meet only once, all day on Saturdays from 10 a.m. to 6 p.m.

The Teer Technology of Soul workshops are designed to give students an opportunity to master effortless, fearless, spontaneous, and powerful communication. These two courses replaced the Pyramid Process One and Two courses and included concepts from the Master Liberation Workshop.

Teer wanted these courses to train the participants to be effective communicators by bridging the psychic distance between audience and stage. Students were to become more comfortable with people in any setting and to make a sincere commitment to becoming whole, complete, self-reliant, fully creative beings.[36] TTS is geared to help all participants regardless of their interests, and some of the participants, in fact, did not plan to become performers but enrolled in the class to gain communicative skills.

When I attended a TTS class in October of 1987, before an evening performance of *The Legacy*, I observed the carry-over from the work in class to the performance. Cast members for *The Legacy* were either in the class or graduates of another NBT class. The exercises involved students singing in front of the class. They sang without accompaniment and without regard to being on key, using only nonsense syllables such as "la la la" or "do do do." The remaining class members had to interpret the song and its message from the movements and expressions which were used. After singing, each performer received a critique from Teer and the class and was given an opportunity to perform the exercise again and to improve on it.

Teer promised the participants that when the classes were completed (1) their confidence would be increased and they would possess the ability to perform in any environment, (2) they would be fortified with boldness and charisma, and (3) their freedom to express themselves as creative beings would be more complete.[37]

Teer intends her Technology of Soul Class to develop a positive self-image that might help her students later in an audition, a speech, or a job interview. She also believes that the class will benefit those who have felt fear, rejection, depression, resentment, or apathy. According to Teer,

> Teer Technology of Soul is designed to improve their [the students'] communicative skills as well as elevate their confidence. It is a catharsis of mind, body and soul, a method of freeing black people enslaved by negative thinking, a cross between Dale Carnegie and Stokely Carmichael.[38]

Some of Teer's aims seem to have been realized, if one may judge from comments from several graduating students quoted in NBT publicity materials in April, 1987:

Greg Hawkins: If you really try, you can get anything you want in this world today. Think about it!

Carleen Jones: I feel an awakening and I feel a lot of energy inside me.

Gordon Easley: My life has opened up tremendously in every respect. I can do anything I want to do.

Carla Small: I think everyone should be aware of the good feelings and the family you feel when you're here and it's great.

Celeste Blackwell: It was actually quite moving to see people get up and be very honest about where they were and where they are and what the program did for them. And I had a good time.

Kevin Morse: It was a great experience being around so many positive Black people who just want to encourage each other. I'm a rookie, a new member and I'm looking forward to being here.[39]

THE IDENTITY, DIGNITY AND TRUST COURSE

I attended the "Identity, Dignity and Trust" course in January, 1988. The class was scheduled from 10:00 a.m. to 6 p.m. on a Saturday, and students were encouraged to arrive early. Participants entering the foyer had their coats taken by graduates of TTS who were there to help. These graduates greeted newcomers, introduced them to everyone, and showed them where fruit and herbal tea were available. In the classroom, Teer sat by a table with a white tablecloth adorned with fresh flowers and incense. The twenty-two class participants sat in a circle facing Teer. She greeted each student by name and also introduced visitors for the students' benefit.

Teer began the class with a physical and vocal warm-up using popular music to establish a rhythm. The students danced and changed partners continually until everyone had had an opportunity to interact with one another. Teer moved freely about the group, offering help and encouragement wherever she felt they were needed. Then each student had to say, "Hey, out there! I've got the feeling!" and to employ a physical action to acknowledge how he was feeling. Some of these actions included throwing up both hands, twisting the body in a suggestive way, turning around, or doing a somersault. When actions were negative or sad, Teer challenged students to explain why their attitude was not more positive and why were they not excited about the new day and being alive.

Each student then took a seat and took notes as Teer lectured:

> Freedom. To be Free means that you are autonomous. We invite you
> to experience a mood of peace. Peace is a conversation without worry
> or doubt. Begin taking all your cues from the *heart*. Ask yourself the
> questions: What do I care about? What are my concerns? What is my
> commitment? . . . Shift your conversations. Move through your life
> from the conversation COMMITMENT. . . . If you operate from your
> commitment, from your heart, from your concerns and caring, you
> immediately become effective in the world. You should speak and
> listen from your commitment. You should shift your conversations.
> And be able to move through your life from the conversation of
> Commitment.[40]

When she was asked what conversations were, Teer explained that they
were "interior verbal exchanges. Everybody talks to himself, whether in
the mind or in the heart, and rather than trying to dismiss such
colloquies, the participant should listen in. In this course, I want you to
reconnect yourself back to a conversation of the heart. I encourage you
to find your commitment in life."[41] These internal conversations take
on the same function as interior monologues taught in Stanislavskian
tradition, the difference being that internal conversations have to do
with real people in life whereas interior monologues are for characters
in a play.

Each participant was encouraged to work fifteen minutes a day at a
"confidence center." Teer defined a confidence center as any space
where the participants could go privately for meditation. Spiritually, it
was a place where they would repeat the following thoughts, supplied
them by Teer:

> You are the Self. You are of God. God's power within you is
> greater than any challenge or circumstance of life. No habit,
> no lifestyle, no personality has the power over you to block
> your full expression of health, prosperity, wisdom, peace and
> joy. The Spirit, the Self, the I Am is great within you. It is a
> divine intelligence, a conversation.[42]

The students were also encouraged to make discoveries of their own. At one session they were asked to describe Africa in as many terms as possible. When Africa was called hot, the students were asked what heat does. They replied that it energizes, breaks up, cleanses, and purifies. Therefore, people from those regions were passionate, big-hearted, praying, creative people. Black people, who had come from Africa, possessed with such attributes.

Teer believed that Black people should not hate White people, for she advocated positive values and considered hate a negative force that could only destroy. Therefore, she taught that one might hate the way people acted or what they had done without hating the people themselves. She also taught that Blacks should associate more with Whites and learn how to live harmoniously with all people. She also instructed her students to be "giantlike." Together with her students, she analyzed the characteristics of giants, and the group determined that giants were tall and therefore far-seeing, that they were able to travel great distances easily, and that they were capable of accomplishing more than the average person. To become giantlike was then to become *their* goal. Therefore, according to Teer, "as NBT liberators, they must look past the obvious, and look for all possible approaches to a problem, and find several solutions; they must move with energy, making sure their bodies were capable of the task."[43]

The students at such classes were usually dismissed for lunch at around one o'clock. They were given an hour to eat but told that they must stay together so as to further the impetus of the morning's work. They usually spent the time congratulating one another on their progress and arranging a time and a meeting place to complete exercises and homework together. Typically, they returned to their seats before the hour was up, eager to continue.

In the second half of the class, the students worked on monologues, scenes, and improvisations. Teer assigned some of the pieces, and others were of the students' own choosing. She would often work with individual students while the others were busy taking notes and writing questions to ask her before the end of the class. She spent the last half hour reviewing the students' progress, assigning other scenes, and answering questions.

THE POWER IN YOU WRITER'S COURSE

A writer's workshop called "The Power in You," begun in May of 1985, offers another instance of the consciousness-raising Teer practices. The class was developed by Veona Thomas, playwright of *Nzinga's Children* and *A Matter of Conscience*, and NBT workshop Program Director Ade Faison. According to a notice in the *Amsterdam News*, the course, "was designed for you to gain certainty and confidence, increase your ability to create and speak powerfully with your own written words in front of a live audience and have your work published by the end of the course."[44] The goal of the workshop is for each participant to write, publish, and market a dramatic work and then have it performed in a showcase production. The student playwrights are given an opportunity to learn word processing in order to produce their manuscripts and manage corrections easily. Their finished work is bound in a booklet and published in a soft cover by The National Black Theatre. Then, students from the performance courses act in the plays, and staff members often serve as directors.

By the end of the course all students are acquainted with professionals who might help them in the future. In keeping with Teer's philosophy of promoting positive values in students, the course also encourages self-expression through its written work and fosters entrepreneurial skills in each student.[45]

THE ENTREPRENEURIAL COURSE

The main purpose of Teer and her assistants in the Entrepreneurial class was to assess her students' talents and to build their marketing skills so that they might become happy and prosperous people.[46] The course involved the students' learning the distinction between being an artist, a manager, and a producer. Conrad Neblett, one of Teer's assistants in the Entrepreneurial program, asserts that the goal of the course "is to fuse art and business so artists can become competent in both business and art."[47] He further maintains that

The NBT's purpose . . . is to make the artist self-sufficient to the point where he or she has the expertise to create their own shows and audiences. What is happening now in the theatre entrepreneur program is that we are learning both business and real estate. If a role doesn't come along with dignity, you have other areas to fall back on.[48]

GRADUATION CEREMONIES

Besides observing a class and a performance, I was able to witness the dress rehearsal and graduation for the Teer Technology of Soul Class on June 24 and 25, 1992. This ceremony was held at Teer's new $12 million edifice, the National Black Theatre's Institute of Action Arts [NBTIAA], where the theatre space is located on the third level and the foyer is decorated with cherry wood totems of the African Gods Shango and Oshun.[49] Windows in the octagonal roof of the building let in the sun. The doors to the theatre space are made from carved wood in the shape of the African deity Obatala, the god of creativity. The floor is covered in blue carpeting donated by Donald Trump.

Upon entering, each participant and guest was asked to remove his shoes. I found the room sparsely decorated except for one small round table decorated with a white tablecloth, fresh flowers in a glass vase, one lit white candle, and burning incense in the vase with the flowers.

There were thirteen students: five male, seven female, eleven of them African-American, and two of them Hispanics. Two drummers entered the space playing djembe drums from Senegal, West Africa. There followed a meditation hour, a quiet time when each participant lay on his back, spread-eagled, eyes closed. At some point the lights went out and the teachers, the brother and sister Abisola and Ade Faison,[50] began chanting. They asked the students to breathe in and let the breath out. At different times participants felt a sprinkle of water brush across their faces as they were asked to rock back and forth and to roll little by little until they touched someone. Then the participants were asked to explore the other body, tickle it, stand, and then look and see the person. Movement began with the drummers shifting the beat, and the group engaged in a live dance or "whip," holding on to another person's hand and moving faster and faster. When they stopped in a semi-circle they began chanting the words "Perfect, Power, God," which crescendoed and moved faster and then decrescendoed.

Next there was a testimony service at which everyone talked about his feelings. Then each sat on the floor and watched a video tape of Teer and the company's 1973 trip to Africa. The video tape showed NBT participants entering the village of Oshogbo and bathing in the Oshun River. After this thirty-minute viewing, the participants rehearsed the actual performance for the TTS graduation.

Rehearsal for the next evening's performance began at 1:30 a.m. Evidently, a pre-arranged program had not been planned. Teer was on the stage with Nabii Faison working on a song with Teer singing and Nabii playing the piano and singing, too. Ade and Abisola Faison worked with the participants on their entrance to the theatre and to the stage.

With the song over, Teer brought the participants on the stage and divided them into three groups of four: the one student left was to become the soloist. Members of each group were given the phrases, "What was it before?" and "How is it now?", and the others were given the phrase "I don't know." These phrases were sung over and over. Teer then taught the group a dance to accompany the musical number.

After this, all the students stood in a straight line on stage to testify. Teer taught a line dance, where the students moved back and forth together. All participants used the same format to testify, which had them saying: "I (participant's name) declare that by (a future date) I will (stating a personal resolution). It is my divine heritage and I will it to be so—Can I get a Witness?" At that point the student gave a "high five" to the next participant.[51]

During this exercise, students who had difficulty with volume, diction, rhythm, or pitch were stopped and made to repeat the exercise until the teachers were satisfied. This became very tedious for the hour was late and the students were tired. However, no one complained and each student tried to help his fellow classmates and encouraged them to "Try again," or "You can do it," or "It's okay, I know you're going to get it right this time." Finally, all were satisfied. Students were dismissed at 4:05 a.m. and told to return to the theatre at 6 p.m. later that day.

Graduation night was itself a theatrical event. The theatre, with a seating capacity of about one-hundred-and-fifty seats, was crowded with friends, relatives, former TTS graduates, members of the Harlem Community, and NBT personnel. Admission for each audience member cost five dollars. The students were lavishly dressed as they entered "steppin'"[52] in single file, and they promenaded all around the theatre before taking the stage. Several students had special presentations: one student had written a poem; one had written a song to sing; the Colombian student gave a special testimony; and another played the saxophone. Throughout the performance, and especially during the testimony service, there was constant interaction between the audience and the performers. Many of the participants were crying, as were members of the audience.

After the services, the students presented Teer and their teachers with gifts. Then refreshments were served, and the participants engaged in conversation with the audience. I could hear the participants saying things like: "I'm glad you encouraged me to take this class." One mother told Teer that she had taken the TTS class and then encouraged all four of her daughters to join, and that this particular daughter was her third. The graduation did not seem like a final event, and the participants talked about what they were going to do next to fulfill their resolutions.

SUMMARY

Classes have from the beginning been the foundation of the NBT. They provide a range of experience for the prospective performer or playwright. In addition to training actors and playwrights, whose compositions the young actors perform, the NBT maintains a complete theatre company.

Above all, Teer focuses on consciousness raising, using community resources in Harlem, and she encourages her students to investigate their own heritage as performers rather than as characters in a play. Teer asserts that the characters that her students will portray can be drawn from the Five Cycles of evolution studied by each student.

Although students in traditional acting classes often hope that some kind of bonding takes place, Teer goes further by involving the students in social functions. The students must attend church, the Apollo, and go to a bar together. If even one student is absent, the activity must be repeated. Having the students extend their instruction outside of the classroom helps them to bond not only with their group but with their culture.

Finally students must involve themselves in community service in order to be performers at the NBT. Teer places particular emphasis on this condition, and she feels that this helps students to understand that their community is important to them and that they are important to their community. Students will then feel bound not only to the NBT but especially to their community.

NOTES

1. "NBT Workshops in Creative Energy," *NY Amsterdam News*, 9 October 1976, D-8.
2. "NBT Conducts Workshop Series," *NY Amsterdam News*, 19 June 1976, D-14.
3. Pearl Primus, *Current Biography: Who's News and Why 1944* (New York: The H. W. Wilson Co., 1945), p. 552.
4. Martha M. Jones, "Barbara Ann Teer's National Black Theatre," Black Creation vol. 3, no. 4, (Summer 1972), 20.
5. Jones, 20.
6. "Barbara Ann Teer and the National Black Theatre, " *Interreligious Foundation for Community Organization* vol. iv, issue 1, (Jan.-Feb. 1972), 4.
7. "NBT Opens New Season," *NY Amsterdam News*, 12 Nov. 1977, D-14.
8. Valerie Harris, "Power Exchange 2: Barbara Ann Teer," in *Third World Women: The Politics of Being Other*, vol. 2 (New York: Heresies Collective, Inc., 1979), 44.
9. "NBT Conducts Workshop Series," *NY Amsterdam News*, 19 June 1976, D-14.
10. Harris, 44.

11. Harris, 44.

12. *NY Amsterdam News*, 12 Nov. 1977, D-14.

13. *NY Amsterdam News*, 12 Nov. 1977, D-14.

14. *NY Amsterdam News*, 12 Nov. 1977, D-14.

15. Harris, 42.

16. Jessica B. Harris, "The Sun People of 125th Street, The National Black Theatre," *The Theatre of Black Americans*, ed. Errol Hill (New York: Applause, 1987), 286.

17. Thomas A. Johnson, "On Harlem Stage, A Spiritual Journey," *New York Times*, 11 May 1971, E-44.

18. Psalm 100: 1-2, 527.

19. Charlie L. Russell, "Barbara Ann Teer: We Are Liberators Not Actors," *Essence* (March, 1971), 49.

20. Russell, 49.

21. "Barbara Ann Teer: Producer," *Ebony*, August 1977.

22. Valerie Harris, 42.

23. Russell, 49.

24. Harris, 286.

25. Russell, 49.

26. Harris, 287.

27. Russell, 49.

28. *Interreligious Foundation for Community Organization*, 4.

29. The Day Care Center remained opened until the March 1983 fire which destroyed their supplies and facilities. Teer states that the day care center will open again in the future.

30. Jones, 20.

31. Tony Best, "Barbara Ann Teer and the Liberators," *NY Amsterdam News* 12 November 1975, D-10.

32. Jones, 20.

33. Best, 10-11.

34. Jones, 20.

35. Jones, 20.

36. Teer Technology of Soul Workshops advertising pamphlet, 1985, 3.

37. Teer Technology of Soul Workshops Pamphlet, 5.

38. Quoted by Bivins, 9.

39. "Accent on New Possibilities," *NBT Magazine* vol. 1, no. 2 (spring-summer, 1987), 8.

40. Barbara Ann Teer, "Freedom," Hand-out sheet from class materials. A copy of this form will be in the appendix.
41. Private interview, 20 January 1988.
42. Barbara Ann Teer, Hand-out sheet from class materials. Available in the appendix.
43. Teer lecture, TTS, 20 January 1988.
44. "NBT Offers Performing Writers Workshop," *NY Amsterdam News*, 1 March 1986, 25.
45. Acting classes were taught by Teer and her staff assistants Ade Faison, Shirley Clemmons Faison, Nabii Faison, and Abisola Faison, or Tunde Samuel, many of whom had been with Teer since the group's beginning. The entrepreneur course was begun in 1987 as a result of Barbara Ann Teer's study with Dr. Fernando Flores, a former Minister of Business and Finance from Chile. The other instructors at the NBT included Ron Renfroe, Ife Saunders, Mamie Mae Stone, Billy Ray Tyson, and Conrad Neblett.
46. In responding to her feelings about the entrepreneur class, Abisola Faison stated that, "The first thing is to develop the human beings . . . . to transform the culture that we live in such a way that we are autonomous, we have dignity and self-respect as artists. After so many years of that you get a company of people who are clear about their identity as African-Americans and who are clear about their purpose and function as artists."
47. Lindsay Patterson, "The National Black Theater Thrives," *Theaterweek* March 28, 1988, 31.
48. Patterson, 31.
49. The art work for Teer's NBTIAA was designed and completed by the artists from Oshogbo, Nigeria. The king of the city sent ten of the village's artists to decorate the theatre. These artists were experts in stone, aluminum, wood, and copper carving. They spent the summer of 1990 completing the decorations for the theatre.
50. In January of 1992 the NBT staff person known as Keibu Faison changed his name to Ade Faison.
51. A high five is defined as one person hitting the open palm of another person with his open palm above the heads of both persons. In Black culture this is a symbol of rejoicing or affirming a point.
52. "Steppin" is a choreographed walk for a group accentuating the beat of the music. This processional has traditional African roots which are also evident in the Pentecostal church. In the African traditions before ceremonies there is a

processional dance from the houses to the performance area. Additionally, during the Pentecostal worship services there is generally a processional for the choir. Both of these processions include choreographed movement to entertain and display conspicuous showmanship.

V

The NBT: The Quintessential Black Theatre of Harlem

> I got to love myself so much
> that I can love you so much
> that you can love you so much
> that you can start loving me!
>
> Barbara Ann Teer, "Black Mantra," 1969

The NBT answers the need established by earlier dramatists who called for a unique Black Theatre in Harlem. It answers that need because (1) it is a Black theatre, (2) its rituals, by and large, were the most successful of all the Black experimental theatres of the 1960s, (3) it has lasted longer than any other Black theatre in Harlem, (4) it has become a cultural treasure in Harlem supported by an audience, and (4) it has become a model for other Black community theatres in America.

The longevity of the NBT stands as one factor in its being declared a model for other community theatres. Since The Lafayette Players, Harlem's first Black theatre in 1915, through the New Lafayette Theatre in 1966, there have been over fifteen community theatres in Harlem, and none has lasted as long as the NBT.

In 1915, the Anita Bush Stock Company was formed to perform plays first at the Lincoln Theatre and later at the Black-owned Lafayette. Although it did not present any Black plays, for few could be found, this company lasted for seventeen years, stopping mainly due to the Great Depression. Loften Mitchell writes that this organization demonstrated,

> one devoted to showing white folks that I, too, can play roles that you think are yours alone, that I, too, am human. It was, in short, a defensive organization, unsure of what might have been unleashed had it said: "I am Black, so what? This is me, and this is my creative effort."[1]

The Lafayette Players helped to establish other theatre companies in Chicago, Baltimore, and Washington, D. C. before folding in 1932.

The Harlem Renaissance helped to inspire many smaller theatre companies in Harlem and all were short lived: W. E. B. DuBois' Krigwa Players, The Harlem Experimental Theatre in 1928, which ceased after eight productions, and in 1929 the Negro Art Theatre and the Harlem Community Theatre who produced one show each. The Dunbar Garden Players, directed by playwright Eulalie Spence ended after only two productions at the St. Mark's Church.

In 1937 Langston Hughes' Harlem Suitcase Theatre featured a bare stage and storytelling techniques but it lasted only a few years. In 1938 the Rose McClendon Players, under the direction of Dick Campbell and his wife, Murial Rahn, dedicated itself to building community theatre. However, when World War II began Campbell was offered a job and other company members were going in the service, so the company disbanded.

In 1940, the American Negro Theatre presented plays in the old Schomburg Library on 137th Street. However, this company lost sight of their original goal after its production of *Anna Lucasta* was moved to Broadway, and it disbanded around 1952.

The 1960s produced another explosion with more than seven theatre companies forming in Harlem. In 1964, the New Heritage Repertory Theatre Company, under the leadership of Roger Furman, formed and was interested in producing Black plays in traditional productions. The company did well until Furman died. Neither the Afro-American Singing Theatre (of which little is known), the Afro-American Studio for Acting and Speech developed by Ernie

McClintock, nor Hazel Bryant's Afro-American Total Theatre, survived into the 1980s.

In 1966, the New Lafayette Theatre began in Harlem under the direction of Robert McBeth and Adam Miller. Mance Williams writes that

> It was the expressed intention of McBeth to bring Black artists into closer contact with the Black community so they could be reoriented to Black life. He viewed the Black community in a national rather than a local sense. There were Black artists and there were Black communities all over the United States, but there was no point at which they could converge and commune together. The New Lafayette would thus become a Mecca to be visited by artists from across the country, who could take back to their communities the inspiration and knowledge gained from their experience. This way, NLT proposed to serve as a "national community theatre."[2]

The company was interested in performing plays about Black life written by Black playwrights, and soon Ed Bullins joined the group. They performed plays written by Bullins and also rituals penned by both McBeth and Bullins. Although they received a large grant, they were unable to maintain themselves in Harlem, and in 1972 they voted themselves out of business.

Teer chose to sacrifice some glory in order to remain in Harlem, rather than moving downtown or changing into an Equity theatre as did the Negro Ensemble Company under Douglas Turner Ward. Changing to an Equity house would mean higher salaries for the actors, and Teer could charge higher ticket prices and possibly generate a higher income. However, Teer feels that this would be an imposition on a community that would have difficulty meeting raised prices. Teer prefers to be subsidized in ways other than by taxing the community.

Much of Teer's approach has involved changing the terminology and definitions used to describe the NBT. She invoked associations in labeling the NBT a "Temple of Liberation, designed to preserve, maintain, and perpetuate the richness of the Black life-style."[3] Teer called the NBT's plays "revivals" or "rituals," and Genevieve Fabre writes that

For the National Black Theatre ritual is a communal event organized and studied, refined and unambiguous. It aims not to bring African ritual into a different context, but to create a ritual that renews the ties among cultural elements alienated from one another.[4]

Teer uses the example of Pentecostal church revivals, but rather than reaffirming the connection between believer and God, she reaffirms the relationship between performer and audience. Jessica Harris asserts that *"Revival* has nothing to do with down-home camp meeting. [It is] a didactic work, but then the major aim of the National Black Theatre is education and nation-building."[5] In the process of nation-building, claims Harris, "The ritual releases a psychic liberating energy; thus Teer calls the actors—liberators."[6] Similarly, Teer labels the audience members "participants" and challenges the limiting concept of a stage as a self-contained performing space. Teer states that

There is no such thing as a stage, nor such a thing as an audience: only liberators and participants. And you try to remove that psychic distance, that nigger space that separates Black people from each other. In a ritual you mold, meet, and merge into one. You feel, laugh, cry, and experience life together.[7]

With distinctions between performers and spectators removed, according to Teer, the audience can relax and become more engaged in the dramatic experience. The performers are also able to relax, and to be more spontaneous and natural in a setting which does not put pressure on them to emote, but rather refuels them with the energy of the participants.

    Teer never forgets her obligation to the audience, for her aim is to "put theatre in the service of the community and define the dialectical relationship between artists and the community as represented by the assembly."[8] Yet she does not see the relation of artist to public as a slavish subservience or as pandering. She recognizes that those who come to the theatre have much to offer the performers besides the price of a ticket. She declares: "The black artist must remember that it is the people that give him light and clarity of vision and who reinforce his sensibilities."[9]

Here again, Teer departs from much traditional theatre in seeking to identify and elaborate ways in which performers may be stimulated by an audience. "Every ritual has a function," she states. "Ours is to open up, liberate, regain and reclaim our spiritual freedom. If we are successful, then people watching will feel this."[10] Teer does not claim that traditional theatre fails to arouse emotion but rather that in traditional theatre feelings come from observing performances, while in the NBT feelings ought to arise from more active kinds of involvement.

CRITICAL RESPONSE TO SELECTED PRODUCTIONS

Next I will focus on one play, *The Legacy* and five original "revivals" performed by the NBT. These include *The Ritual: To Regain Our Strength and Reclaim Our Power*, 1970; *A Revival: Change/Love Together/ Organize!*, 1972; *Soljourney into Truth: A Ritualistic Revival*, 1974; *Softly Comes a Whirlwind Whispering in Your Ear*, 1978; *Soul Fusion*, 1980; and *The Legacy*, 1988. The "revivals" represent Teer's first attempt at formulating her type of theatre, while *The Legacy* represents her attempt to adapt a traditional script to her vision. (A detailed synopsis of each play is available in the appendix.)

Each "revival" used different ways of greeting the audience as they entered the performance space. This could happen as simply as it did in *The Ritual*, when the company began "their performance by shaking hands and chatting with the audience,"[11] or as engagingly as it did during *The Revival*, "when the audience, upon entering the theater, encounters the players head on, face to face: beggars after some change [money] . . . [or] a sister totally wrecked by heroin looking to turn a fast two dollar trick."[12] Hazziezah, reviewing for the *Amsterdam News*, wrote that such action was "a far cry from the 'star on the door', 'see my agent'—demeanor of many actors. . . . The beaming smiles of the NBT family remind us that actors and 'stars', if you will, are only real people."[13] The NBT enjoys giving personal touches to its opening sequences so as to lessen aesthetic distance in the theatre. Mauby, after viewing *A Soljourney into Truth* in Trinidad, wrote:

Each individual is greeted personally, the first contact made as his hand is warmly shaken, his eye firmly held. He is told a little about the show, and asked if he is game [consenting] to participate. If he expresses any doubts, these are smoothed away. All that is asked for is an affirmation of willingness to co-operate. The psychology behind this approach is neat. The physical barrier has now been broached without fuss, and further contact has a comforting precedent.[14]

Besides such greetings, each "revival" also included singing and dancing and the use of instruments such as "conga drums, guitars and tambourines."[15] A piano or synthesizer was used as well, for, according to Harris, "Music is an integral part of the performances at Ms. Teer's theatre, as is dance and movement."[16] Although these elements can be present in Eurocentric productions, Harris notes that "music and movement are thought of in the African sense and are integrated within the performance, flowing naturally out of the situation that is being presented."[17]

Chanting was also used during "ritual" performances, and Hazziezah suggests that "While the cast was chanting . . . it occurred to me that perhaps the same message of the Sixties is needed again today at the height of the apathy of the Seventies."[18] On the other hand, Lionel Mitchell noted that *Softly Comes a Whirlwind Whispering in Your Ear* had less chanting. He wrote that "Experimentation has paid off and the years when pretty girls seemed to seize every opportunity to chant 'Afrika!' 'Africa!' to the point of delirium have given way to a harvest of very masterful, naturalistic (even impressionistic!) theatre."[19]

The most impressive element of the "revivals," however, according to critics, was the energy exuded by the group. Michael Givens asks, "You want energy? Their energy, it may be told, is African heredity along with 'sources of the sun.'"[20] Clayton Riley reports that *The Revival* "works best when it is exploring the defiant, stubbornly energetic life style existing on America's torn and wasted inner city streets."[21] Albert DeLeon felt an abundance of energy from this same production in writing that "When the first act is over, one is raised to such an intense level of excitement that it seems impossible for the second act to sustain that sensation. It does. Indeed, the second act raises one's involvement with the show even higher.'[22] Charles Burden testifies that *Softly Comes a Whirlwind Whispering in Your Ear*'s "simple story line serves as a touchstone for cast and audience to generate a certain energy together and create a certain atmosphere."[23] Such excitement and enthusiasm was also evident to Larry Conley who in reviewing *Soljourney Into Truth* revealed that "as theater the NBT mixture of love, African ritualism and positive thinking makes for a genuinely exhilarating evening."[24] Vigorous action has been one of the NBT's most impressive achievements.

One other important similarity in all "revivals" is the opportunity for audience interaction during each performance, sometimes planned and sometimes spontaneous. In the early "revivals" there was space for "testifying" not only from the performers but also from the spectators. *The Ritual* ends with the audience together on stage dancing and singing together,[25] while according to DeLeon, *The Revival*'s "structure is such that there is room for improvisation by the performers to an extent that they are allowed to become personal with the audience, creating a tremendously inspirational atmosphere for everyone."[26] Here the audience was entertained and uplifted not only by the performers but by the other "participants" as well.

Although all performances of revivals contained audience interaction, the shows were not always successful in prompting such reactions. After a performance of *Soljourney into Truth*, Mauby reported that "the show does depend on a measure of reluctance to participate. Immediate total co-operation by the whole audience could finish 'Soljourney' in less time."[27]

"Whirlwind" had a decidedly different effect on its audience. Charles Burden writes that

> The final act is the performance of this concert for which she [Iansa, the main character] has been rehearsing. The part of the audience is played by—yes, you guessed it—the audience. Thus, from beginning to end, audience and cast switch back and forth between "play" and "reality."[28]

Lionel Mitchell praises "the opening scenes . . . which are perhaps the most emotionally rich spontaneous ensemble ever put on stage."[29] Such remarks suggest that the story line of *Whirlwind* was more focused and detailed than those of *The Ritual* or *Soljourney into Truth*.

Special greetings, music, singing, dancing, chanting, high energy, audience interaction, and spontaneity were elements which engaged the NBT's audience in unusual ways. Some elements were not as successful as others in their implementation, but each distinguished the NBT as a group which entertained its audience in ways not always familiar in the American professional theatre.

BLACK THEATRICAL ELEMENTS IN NBT PRODUCTIONS

In the 1960s and 1970s Black writers began writing revolutionary plays, which were professionally produced and thus reviewed by professional critics. However, they found the critics both excessive and obtuse, finding fault with the structure, meaning, and directing of these plays but missing more of what the writers regarded as the salient points of the productions. What was missing from these plays was an interpreter to bridge the cultural gap. One interpreter, Margaret Wilkerson, felt what was needed was Black theorists who could suggest criteria by which plays written by blacks could be judged. Wilkerson writes that Black theatre is "communal, functional and participatory," for "productions which feature Black casts in plays relating to their lives have an instant community—not spectators, but a spiritual community."[30]

Wilkerson expands on other differences between traditional and Black theatrical standards. She writes that

> Many Black theatres of the 1960s and 1970s are . . . consciously developing a theatre which relates intimately to the desires and needs of its community in many and varied ways. Triumph amidst adversity, the dangers of narcotic addiction, the joy and struggle of male/female relationships, [and] the spiritual poverty of assimilationism are only a few of the themes being explored in these community theatres. There are significant experiments which tap

African culture for viable combinations of music, dance, mime, and storytelling.[31]

Wilkerson believes that these are areas in which Black theatre differs markedly from traditional Western theatre, and the NBT productions manifest each area of Wilkerson's model.

The triumph-amid-adversity theme suggested by Wilkerson can be seen in the story line of *Softly Comes a Whirlwind Whispering in Your Ear*. The ritual tells the story of Iansa, who although afraid to sing anything but opera professionally, decides to make one popular concert appearance to raise funds to get her father out of jail. After this debut, she "discovers her real value as a singer can be used as a political tool to spread the message of freedom and truth within the medium of music, for more than just one night, for more than just one father."[32] The message of *Softly Comes a Whirlwind*, according to Curt Davis, "is for anybody and everybody, black and white, and *Whirlwind* was created not so much for theatrical reasons as social and philosophical ones. It whispers in the eternal still small voice of the power for change within us all."[33] Teer stresses that adversity can make people strong and that "Criticism should be positive."[34] All the NBT productions ended on a positive note with singing and hand-holding.

Nevertheless, the NBT's themes were also serious and socially relevant, another feature of Black theatre identified by Wilkerson. The NBT's second ritual, *A Revival,* treated the dangers of narcotic addiction. This revival featured the life of Porky, a drug addict who owed money to Walt, his supplier. Unable to pay, Porky was physically beaten by Walt. He was then befriended by Toussaint, a former prisoner but more recently the leader of the Temple of Liberation. Through a special service, Porky was healed of his wounds and exhorted not to return to that life but to work for positive Black change. Albert DeLeon writes:

> This production presents the Black lifestyle at its worst— pimps, hustlers, pushers, prostitutes, junkies—and confronts the viewer, in microcosmic form, with a situation which has a divisive and destructive effect on the Black community. . . . "A Revival" is successful in magnifying an acute problem infecting the Black

community and by doing so, emphasizing the need for something to be done to terminate this disease.[35]

A *CUC* critic wrote that "the NBT is specifically attempting to use theatre in a religio-magical way, to move blacks to a revulsion of such 'negatives' as drugs, drink, and self-abuse and to awaken such 'positives' as cultural pride, racial identity, and self-respect."[36] Teer believes that her works serve a dual purpose, not only exposing the wrong but showing its remedy as well. The *Amsterdam News* reported that *The Revival*

> gathered its tension from the conflict between dope pushers and their struggle with a new religio-nationalist movement in the community which attempts to free the junkies and their ilk from the wrong influences by teaching the unfortunates who they are and surplanting their despair with a more positive program.[37]

The positive influences in these productions were not always imposed from above or from without. They were sometimes found in "the joy and struggle of male/female relationships," another point on Wilkerson's list of ways in which Black theatre can connect to the Black community. The NBT has, on occasion, exposed the forces that exist outside the male/female relationship and demonstrated how the unity of the relationship helps to solve the problems. In *Softly Comes a Whirlwind*, Iansa is helped by a male friend Ajire, who wants her to go on to bigger and better things. In *Soul Fusion*, Jack Henry Bruwell, a pessimist trying to save his theatre, is advised by his woman friend, Rebecca Branch, to "be self-reliant and seek independent ownership of the institution."[38] The NBT has continuously worked to solidify relationships between Black men and women.

As Wilkerson says of Black theatre in general, the NBT's rituals show "the spiritual poverty of assimilationism" and the necessity of finding inner sources of self-validation. The NBT's first ritual found this theme in its subtitle, *To Regain Our Strength and Reclaim Our Power*. Teer says that

The whole thing is just a shift in conceptualizing the concept of culture. . . . Why Black culture in the world is probably the most lucrative phenomenon or commodity in the whole world. In Africa, Black America . . . James Brown. They reign. . . . You know people want to give up their culture and to adopt ours. It's because we've combined the primitive, meaning the first, with the 'civilized-technologized' which might be the last . . . and come out with something unique, Black American! And it is profound![39]

Teer favors a celebration of blackness as a theme for her ideology, training, and productions. Having Blacks understand the richness of their culture validates them and helps to restore their self-esteem, she believes.

Wilkerson also argues that "theatre is similar to the Black church and serves the historical function of a place where Black people can be in the majority, away from the scrutiny or imposition of outsiders."[40] All of Teer's rituals have the flavor of the church. During the performance I witnessed of *The Legacy*, when one of the gospel numbers became particularly emotional, the piano player jumped up and started shouting. Other audience members joined in clapping and saying, "Yeah," "Praise Him," and "Hallelujah." No one seemed surprised or expressed any negative opinions about this interruption of the production. This church-like atmosphere pleased the audience. One *Amsterdam News* reporter wrote after viewing *The Revival* that,

The music and form of this experience [are] very often rooted in the mode of the gospel Black Church. The content is secular. Sometimes an Africanic religious essence is placed in this new- world form. The re-working of our church heritage forms to hold a powerful secularized and theatricalized message is an important part of National Black Theatre's experimentation— expressing an intelligent respect for the Afro-American traditions as well as those of the ancestral land.[41]

Teer wanted all of her productions to be similar to the Pentecostal church services so that people could leave feeling fulfilled, and in a familiar way.

At the same time, however, NBT performances educated their audiences, familiarizing them with their cultural heritage. This again fulfills one of the functions of Black theatre as Wilkerson defines it: the inclusion of some type of African cultural expression via music, dance, mime, or storytelling. *The Ritual*, according to Thomas Johnson, "ended with a revival-like finale—with both liberators and audience members together in the performing space dancing, clapping hands, and singing together, 'We are an African people, together we can change this mixed-up land.'"[42] During the performance of *The Revival*, there is a "descent of the goddess Oshun, Yoruba goddess of Love."[43] The third revival, *Soljourney into Truth*, includes a portion which is "in the form of a fantastic African ritual, the so-called ship 'takes off.' Adeyemi, with a feathered headdress and African garb, appears as a chieftain to whom gifts are brought."[44] African themes weave themselves consistently through the NBT's ritualistic revivals.

Another element of African heritage is improvisation, a vital aspect of every NBT performance. Wilkerson explains the art of improvisation as it relates to the Black theatrical production. She maintains that

> Sometimes traditional theatre dictates containment and control to an audience: the separation of audience from performers, the written text of the play which discourages improvisation, and other elements make many European-American productions fixed events whose form, down to the last detail, is frozen in rehearsal.[45]

Ortiz M. Walton, a Black literary theorist of the 1970s, writes that

> The art of improvisation first found expression in Africa. This can be seen as a natural development in a culture that encouraged free expression of emotion through art. The accent culturally and aesthetically was on spontaneity. Spontaneity in turn means to express feelings as they occur.[46]

Walton argues that the spontaneity and improvisational aspects of theatre are of African origin and the NBT uses them in every performance. The call-and-response method is also employed in many of Teer's productions.

Abiodun Jeyifous agrees generally with Wilkerson's description of Black theatre, but he adds that "The avowed aim of Black theatre is to raise the consciousness of Black people to an awareness of who they are," for "consciousness replaced sensibility as the basic parameter of black theatre criticism."[47] Here, too, the NBT fits the model with its goal to "raise the level of consciousness through liberating the spirits and strengthening the mind of its people."[48] The notion of spiritual rebirth is confirmed in the accounts of every reviewer. Of the NBT's first revival, Johnson wrote that the "final message of the Ritual is that if blacks are to progress, they must utilize a variety of programs, disciplines and approaches, including politics, economics, cultural expressions and aims."[49] *The Revival*, according to *Amsterdam News* critic Clarence Allsopp, offers " a message of love, change and organization of Black folks for positive goals . . . a beautiful African goddess appears at intervals to remind Black people 'We are children of the gods of Africa so be proud of your heritage.'"[50] DeLeon, viewing the same ritual in 1972, wrote that at *The Revival* "everyone was moved by the characters talking about what it is to be Black, and how blacks can better utilize their resources in order to strengthen all that is Black." When Mauby reviewed *Soljourney into Truth,* he clearly identified the message of raising consciousness: "The real purpose of the show, is to teach self-appreciation, how to love yourself, whoever you are, how to 'expand your ability to feel good about being who you are because you are perfect.'"[51]

Charles Burden, writing for *News World*, affirmed that *Softly Comes a Whirlwind Whispering in Your Ear*, the NBT's fourth revival,

> is about supportativeness in human relationships or about people acknowledging their own and others' true value, [for] one actually experiences *as a participant* the interplay of positivity between all present in that upper room, not as "players and audience" but as human beings.[52]

In writing about *The Legacy*, Kelly-Marie Berry acknowledged that the play's "message for African-Americans [was] to unify to meet the struggles and perils of moving forward into the 21st Century."[53] By raising the conscious level of its audience, the NBT felt that it gave its members ammunition against racism, by having them feel good about themselves and spurring them to remember where they came from.

Jeyifous lists three significant aspects of the Black revolutionary theatre movement: 1) to completely reject commercial theatre, its values and its presumed esthetic premises; 2) to allow only the community to validate the plays which directly speak to their life; and 3) to have productions, interpreted only by critics who understand the ideology and aspirations of the group. Teer stated that her rituals were in direct contrast to the Western tradition, which she saw as materialistic as opposed to the Black tradition which she saw as spiritual. When any aspect of performance at the NBT differed from Western theatrical traditions, the difference was often aimed at engaging the audience more fully in performance.

The NBT conforms to the goals of Black theatre as set down by Wilkerson and Jeyifous. However, the NBT's accomplishments transcend these goals, for the NBT has become a cultural institution of stature and influence in the Harlem community. The NBT not only reflects the culture around it; it reflects wholesomely *upon* that culture, giving back an improved though never merely idealized image of Black life, an image strengthened by confidence in the value of the individual. Teer states,

> I submit that this problem of discrimination will continue until we start cultural movements where people get clear about the value of who they are and what they offer to the world so I have built such an institution in Harlem. It's on the corner of Fifth Avenue and 125th Street. We have just built a brand new $10 million facility where our people can come and create freely regardless of race, creed and color. It is from this center of cultural healing that a new entrepreneurial and innovative artist and leader will emerge.[54]

The NBT provides validation for all members of its community. The presence of its building in the community is a constant reminder of a theatre company which supports the community and is supported by it.

Teer and the NBT constantly receive validation from the community in the form of numerous awards. In 1973, she received an AUDELCO Recognition Award for her pioneering work with the NBT, and in 1974 she received a Certificate of Achievement from the Harlem Chamber of Commerce. In 1983, Teer received the Monarch Merit Award for outstanding contributions to the performing and visual arts from the National Council for Culture and Art. And again in 1983, after the fire, the NBT collected over 17,000 signatures from Harlem residents on petitions for restoration funds from New York State.[55]

Because the NBT meets broad criteria for standing as a Black theatre, it fulfills the goal of W. E. B. DuBois for a theatre which is by, for, about, and near Black people. Because it is self-contained, with playwrights, performers, training, and a permanent theatre, it fulfills the need described by Langston Hughes. Because the NBT uses each performance to raise the level of consciousness, to clarify issues, and to entertain, it fulfills the need of a Black theatre as prescribed by Ed Bullins.

The ritualistic revivals conducted by Teer were visions of spectacle aimed at enlightening and inspiring the audience. Each performance was a celebration of life, of identity, and artistic expression. Most critics see Teer as a caring, devoted, talented, and exceptional woman. Her vision has been of a theatre group with immense energy which inspires its audience to support its programs. This audience, in turn, sees the NBT as an important force in the Harlem community, it is the quintessential Black theatre of Harlem.

NOTES

1. Loften Mitchell, *Black Drama: The Story of the American Negro in the Theatre* (New York: Hawthorn Books, Inc., 1967), p. 70.

2. Mance Williams, *Black Theatre in the 1960s and 1970s: A Historical-Critical Analysis of the Movement* (Westport, Connecticut: Greenwood Press, 1985), p. 54.

3. Quoted in Jessica B. Harris, "The National Black Theatre: The Sun People of 125th Street, " in *The Theatre of Black Americans* ed. Errol Hill (New York: Applause, 1987), 283

4. Genevieve Fabre, *Drumbeats, Masks, and Metaphor* (Cambridge, Massachusetts: Harvard University Press, 1983), p. 231.

5. Harris, 289.

6. Harris, 286.

7. Charlie L. Russell, "Barbara Ann Teer: We Are Liberators Not Actors," *Essence* (March 1971), 50.

8. Martha M. Jones, "Barbara Ann Teer's National Black Theater," *Black Creation* vol. 3, no. 4 (Summer 1972),19.

9. Quoted in Charlie L. Russell, "Barbara Ann Teer: 'We are Liberators not Actors,'" *Essence* March 1971, 50.

10. Thomas A. Johnson, "On Harlem Stage, A Spiritual Journey," *New York Times* 11 May 1971, E-44.

11. Hazziezah, "NBT's 'Ritual' to awaken 'Sun People,'" *NY Amsterdam News* 12 November 1977, D-9.

12. Clayton Riley, "Face to Face With the Junkies," *New York Times* 17 Sept. 1972, D-14.

13. Hazziezah, D-9.

14. Mauby, "A Powerful Journey Into Truth," *Trinidad Guardian* 18 December 1975,1.

15. Johnson, E-44.

16. Harris, 285.

17. Harris, 285.

18. Hazziezah, D-9.

19. Lionel H. Mitchell, "NBT Scores With Whirlwind," *NY Amsterdam News* 6 Jan. 1979, 15.

20. Givens, 34.

21. Riley, 2.

22. Albert DeLeon, "Can There Be A Revival?," *The Black American* 11 Sept. 1972, 11.

23. Charles Burden, "'Whirlwind' is Not Just a Play, It's a Happening," *NY News World* 2 May 1980, 27.

24. Larry Conley, "NBT: Theater of Soul," *City Scope Journal of Columbia University* 1976, 54.

25. Johnson, E-44.

26. DeLeon, 11.

27. Mauby, 1.

28. Burden, 27.

29. Mitchell, 15.

30. Margaret Wilkerson, "Critics, Standards and Black Theatre," *The Theatre of Black Americans* ed. Errol Hill (New York: Applause, 1987), p. 320.

31. Wilkerson, p. 321-22.

32. Curt Davis, "Drama Reviews: Softly Comes a Whirlwind—Whispering in Your Ear," *Other Stages* 17 April 1980, 3.

33. Davis, 3.

34. Quoted in Curtiss E. Porter, "THIS HERE CHILD IS NAKED AND FREE AS A BIRD: AN ANNOTATED INTERVIEW WITH BARBARA ANN TEER," *Black Lines*, 2:3 (Spring 1973). Herein will be listed as Teer interview by Porter.

35. DeLeon, "Can There Be A Revival?," *The Black American* 11 September 1972.

36. M.S., *CUC*, 2 Dec. 1972.

37. "'A *Revival*', a Spiritual, African -Play on the stage of National Black Theater," *NY Amsterdam News*, 7 October 1972.

38. Yusef A. Salaam, "'Soul Fusion' Inspires community Control thro' Community Theatre," *NY Amsterdam News* 12 June 1982, 36.

39. Teer interview by Porter.

40. Wilkerson, 321.

41. "'A *Revival*', a Spiritual, African Play on the Stage of National Black *Theater,*" *NY Amsterdam News* 7 Oct. 1972.

42. Johnson, E-44.

43. Jessica B. Harris, "The National Black Theatre: The Sun People of 125th Street," in *The Theatre of Black Americans*, 288.

44. Larry Conley, 53.

45. Wilkerson, 321.

46. Ortiz M. Walton, "A Comparative Analysis of the African and the Western Aesthetics," T*he Black Aesthetic,* ed. Addison Gayle, Jr. (New York: Doubleday and Co., Inc., 1971), 154.

47. Abiodun Jeyifous, "Black Critics on Black Theatre in America," in *The Black Theatre in America*, 328.

48. Jessica B. Harris, p. 284.

49. Johnson, 44.

50. Clarence Allsopp, "The National Black Theatre Gets Set to Revive Harlem," *NY Amsterdam News*, 22 July 1972, D-1.

51. Mauby, "A Powerful Journey into Truth" *Trinidad Guardian* 18 Dec. 1975, 1.

52. Burden, 2.

53. Kelly-Marie Berry, "The Legacy: Memories of the Gospel Song," *Metro Exchange* (August, 1987), 11.

54. "The Issue Is Race," mod. Phil Donahue, *MacNeil/Lehrer News Hour* PBS, WNET, New York, 15 Sept. 1992, pp. 462-63.

55. "The National Black Theatre Milestones," Publicity Material from the National Black Theatre.

Conclusion

This study resounds with the words of Teer's announcement to the world in general and Blacks in particular that

> We are a race of people with a dual cultural heritage. . . . We are American with an African ancestry! . . . [O]ur best and most realistic hope is to go back home, back to the Black community, and begin to build a "new theatre."[1]

This declaration marked her departure from Broadway during the height of her career. The more Teer involved herself in "traditional" theatre on Broadway, the more disillusioned she became by the racism, the prejudice, and the double standard, especially among Whites who were insensitive to her Blackness. She also had difficulty understanding the relevancy of White plays to her life and the relevancy of the actor training she had received to the demeaning roles she was offered. White culture as a whole left her empty, still wanting more, seeking more, feeling unfulfilled. She stated

> I noticed that all the Western theatrical methods that I had been taught were not relevant to Blacks because Blacks come from a different emotional level. Western methods require that one act from the head and people of African descent communicate naturally from the heart. . . . [Western] techniques are based on the intellect, not the soul. The creation of a new form was needed defined by the heart and

soul of Afro-Americans, a form to fit the sensibility and experience of Blacks.[2]

Teer based her theatre on her feelings; she did not know exactly what she wanted, but she wanted a theatre that made her feel comfortable and validated her existence. In 1968 she had only peripheral knowledge of Black Pentecostalism and Yoruba ritual. It was happenstance that the same elements which pacified her theatrically existed within these two distinct institutions which, having historical linkage, knew little of each other. In them she felt the two halves of her heritage as an African-American had come together, the Black Pentecostal worship rites representing the American side and the Yoruba ritual representing the African side. With the discovery of this connection, Teer felt that she had at last locked her sights on a target, that (in the words of her 1968 pronouncement) she was at last on her way "back home."

As she began this journey, she found herself in the company of many others who likewise rejected Broadway and conventional types of theatre. However, any alliance at that time between Blacks and Whites in theatrical theory was rendered improbable by the "social and political tensions associated with the struggle for civil rights" in the 1950s, tensions that increased Blacks' "questioning of values and standards"[3] and made them determined to make a separate place for themselves. And yet, initially at least, the multiplicity of experimental theatre in the 1960s demonstrates how widespread was the discontent with tradition. "Experimental theatres," according to Brockett, "shared a rejection of technocratic society, whether Western or Soviet, and a belief that only the alienated see clearly the problems of society and have the incentive to insist on change."[4] More specifically, Richard Schechner explained that these theatres were rebelling against the kind of theatre which segregated the audience from the performers, had fixed and regular seating for audiences, and had constructed scenery situated in only one part of the theatre.

Teer, too, sought to break down the barriers between performers and audience, barriers which the accretions of centuries had erected in Eurocentric theatre. Teer herself seems to have perceived her goal as escape from all elements of White theatre. Ed Bullins best articulates her argument that the Black experimental theatres were "working towards something entirely different and new that encompasses the soul and spirit of Black people," rather than a "higher form of white art in black faces."[5] Brockett likewise emphasizes the separateness of the Black reaction to White theatrical tradition:

> The "black arts movement" of the 1960s differed from its predecessors in accepting the integrity and dignity of the African American experience and in its unwillingness to compromise with white sensibilities as the price for success. Ultimately, the difference lay in a change in African-American consciousness—toward a firm belief in the worth of "blackness" and all it entailed."[6]

Yet similarities existed between Teer's experiments and experimental theatre in general in the 1960s. She advocated a theatre which appealed to her sensibilities as an African-American. However, the specific steps she took to satisfy her sensibilities were remarkably similar to the axioms that Schechner outlines for environmental theatres. These included the sharing of space by performers and spectators, a flexible environment, simultaneous action possibly in different areas, the unimportance of following a performance text, and production elements which could serve as language rather than only using words.[7] Teer used a performance text, but it was not always the final authority. Her encouragement of spontaneous action by the performers in accordance with or in response to reaction by the spectators caused the text to be constantly adapted. Teer paid particular attention to costumes, and the more grandiose they were, the better. Spectacle was important and special attention was given to props because they were easily handled and removed from the acting space by the performers.

Finally, it was important to Teer to please the audience and to make them feel better. The performance was a celebration as well as a learning experience. The overriding goal of NBT members was to make salient points which might raise the level of consciousness of their audience. Using a performance text which educated Blacks about Blackness was the major difference in Teer's and Schechner's theatres. Teer's revivals also used Act I to demonstrate a particular problem of the Black community while Act II to provide a workable solution.

Additionally, advocating spectacle and a call-and-response element to her performances differed from Schechner's productions.

Judith and Julian Beck's Living Theater was one which promoted poetic drama with improvisation. Starting in 1946 it progressed toward a radical political stance while living a nomadic and communal existence. Sometimes the performers of this theatre were rude and hostile to their audience, insulting them, hurling obscenities, and being disorderly. On the contrary, the NBT's goals included helping the audience to understand themselves; insulting the audience and other negative behavior were thought improper ways of reaching such goals. Furthermore, the NBT's role in the Harlem community for twenty-five years also ruled out a nomadic existence. More importantly, Teer was not interested in non-realistic improvisation. Teer's concern was for heightened realistic performances. Though both were political, the Living Theatre focused more on human rights while the NBT concentrated on the rights of African-Americans.

Another experimental theatre, the Open Theatre, bears certain similarities to Teer's experiment but differs, again, in instructive ways. Joseph Chaikin and Peter Feldman started the Open Theatre in 1963. Upset over approaches to acting, they abandoned "unnecessary" theatrical elements, which included costumes, make-up, props, and scenery. Although they used improvisation and minimal lighting, they did not interact with the audience. The Open Theatre's policy of abandoning theatrical elements and providing a minimalist atmosphere would have restrained the goal of Teer's theatre to exhilarate the emotions through the heightening effect of an extraordinary atmosphere.

The Polish Laboratory Theatre, Jerzy Grotowski's experimental theatre which started in the late 1950s, similarly exhibited elements of resemblance to the NBT. Built upon the concept of theatre as a ritualized communal experience, the Polish Laboratory Theatre attempted to reproduce for its audiences a primal tribal ceremony that liberated the spiritual energy of the congregation or tribe. Labeled as a "poor theatre," it eliminated everything absolutely unnecessary for production. With make-up completely forbidden, the costumes, props, scenery, and lighting were chosen for functionalism as opposed to decoration. Great attention was placed on acting and strenuous physical training was required. During productions, however, it discouraged any audience participation or improvisation by the performers.

It would be unfair to suggest that the experimental theatres which sprang up and sank into obscurity were failures while the endurance of the NBT proves its success. It may, in fact, be truer to say that the NBT has lasted precisely because its ultimate goal has yet to be fully achieved: the liberation of an oppressed minority's soul. On the other hand, the special urgency of this quest has much to do with the NBT's survival. Teer's endeavor amounts to a long-overdue assertion of the identity of Black Americans, and her rejection of White standards is a rejection of the "masking" people of color have often had to do.

Similar to Teer's quest is El Teatro Campesino's. It represents a minority experimental theatre working against discrimination that also uses ritual, religion, improvisation and a political focus. Luis Valdez founded the theatre in 1965 to dramatize the issues of the grape pickers' strike and to encourage other workers to join that union. After meeting its initial purpose, El Teatro Campesino moved to raise the consciousness of Mexican-Americans by giving more information on their heritage during performances, including Mexican myths and incidents of discrimination against Mexican-Americans by the United States.

Valdez' theatre provides interesting parallels to Teer's NBT. Both were bilingual, El Teatro in Spanish and English and the NBT in Black colloquialism and English. Both used a traditional style of folk theatre more concerned with "process" than "product." Both were concerned with their audience, although the NBT invited spontaneous and interruptive outbursts from its audience, while El Teatro usually had discussions with the audience after performances. Whereas Valdez often used myths, Teer mostly used events from the present. Both theatres had a religious grounding, with El Teatro concerned for a Catholic and Indian heritage, and the NBT concerned with Black Pentecostals and African heritage. Once again, the parallels of the NBT and El Teatro Campesino are parallels with distinct differences.[8]

Teer seems to have drawn ideas from each of these experimental theatres; however, she denies any knowledge of these theatres or their views. She merely says, "Did they perform in Harlem? Well, I don't know them." To Teer any similarities are by accident rather than design, for her main objective (in Brockett's words) was "wholly rejecting white culture" and she and other Blacks of the 1960s "sought to create a black arts movement completely removed from the white context."[9] This removal, for Teer, meant physically moving to Harlem, a dominantly Black environment, in order to maintain a communal existence in Harlem, away from White culture, and to embrace the contributions of African-Americans in Harlem where most businesses were Black-owned. Moreover, the Black Pentecostal churches of Harlem brought Teer a feeling of home, a place where [they could be] and the NBT company could "relax and be colored in speech, movement, and behavior patterns, a theatre where you are free to experiment and create."[10]

However, Teer was not the first to incorporate religious traditions in ritualistic theatre. Throughout history many cultures have maintained a bond between religion and theatre. Brockett records that the origins of theatre were sowed during religious festivals to honor the god Dionysus. Roman theatrical performances were usually during an official religious festival also honoring various gods. During the Middle Ages, many countries witnessed dramas stemming from stories, miracles, and passages from the Bible. Brockett writes that religious plays of the Medieval era treated the triumph of virtue and the punishment of vice within an eternal order and that farces showed an imperfect man within the social order.[11]

Africa had also forged bonds between its religious ceremonies and theatrical entertainments. John Mbiti reports that the single most important difference between Western and African religious theatrical ceremonies was that for the Africans, religion and theatre were synonymous. He writes: "Religion is the African's celebration of life and his source of survival, whereas traditional theatre is his way of giving witness to this."[12] For the African, religion and theatre are both free, communal, and a celebration of life which can instruct, entertain, please, or provoke into action. Both theatre and religion are carriers of the culture among its people.

Religion exerted the greatest influence upon the thinking and living of the people concerned, for "wherever Africans are, so is their religion."[13] Religion was the African's celebration of life and his source of survival. In the traditional African community there are no irreligious people, for to be human is to belong to the whole community and to belong to the community, is to be involved, fully participating in the beliefs, customs, ceremonies, rituals, and festivals of that community.

For Teer and her theatre, the community holds the same importance. Her theatre is concerned with the needs, problems, and interests of the community and what answers, solutions, and balms they may need. As religion played an important role in the theatres of the past, it is now injecting new life into theatre again, but this time in Harlem. Although others used religion as a source before, Teer is the first to combine the African celebrative rites and the Black Pentecostal ceremonial worship elements as the basis for a theatre.

Thus, it is not surprising that the National Black Theatre has remained a viable resource in the Harlem Community. In 1974 the NBT received a Certificate of Achievement from the Harlem Chamber of Commerce for its contributions as an institution of cultural awareness. The Mayor of New York, Edward Koch, and the Governor of New York, Hugh L. Carey, declared May 7, 1979 to be National Black Theatre Day to "direct the citizens of New York to the outstanding achievement of the National Black Theatre," citing that the "international acclaim won by the NBT has brought great credit to New York."[14] The NBT won the Community Service Award in 1980 from Reality House, Inc. to celebrate Harlem Week. Over 2,000 Harlem residents attended this event and witnessed the traditional ruler of the Yoruba Empire of Ile-Ife, Nigeria, King Alaiyeluwe Oba Okunde Sijuwade, bequeath to Teer $5,000 as a declaration of his continued support for the NBT's efforts. In 1983 The National Council for Culture and Art bestowed the Monarch Merit Award upon Teer and the NBT for their contributions to Harlem. Also in 1983, after the fire which destroyed its facility, over 17,000 Harlem residents signed a petition demanding funding to restore the Theatre. Today the theatre is one of the few cultural treasures remaining in Harlem, surviving the Apollo, the Savoy, the Lafayette Theatre, and the American Negro Theatre.

The NBT continues to choose and devise its productions in response to the Harlem community. For all their revivals, Teer and her students developed questionnaires which they took to the community, and the community's answers formed the foundations for the first act of those revivals. They listened to the community to help identify problems, and they searched for answers to those problems which they then developed into the second acts of those revivals. Today, Tunde Samuel still listens to the members of the Harlem community to ascertain what they are interested in, and he provides plays and musicals which interest the community. Having heard, for example, the Harlem Community discuss (and not discuss) homosexuality, Samuel quickly found two plays, *Face to Face* and *Third Rhythm*, which dealt with that issue.

Much of the training offered presently at the NBT promotes self-worth and individual wholeness. It helps African-Americans feel good about themselves, and it can help any minority that has been made to feel inferior by cultural hegemony or racial tensions. As we move toward the twenty-first century, Teer's training becomes especially helpful to professional theatres and universities in further understanding African-Americans and other minorities as well.

Living in a culturally hegemonic society means that institutions are dominated by one cultural group. The only way this can be changed is for the dominant culture to appropriate more from each subordinate culture. Once this has happened, perhaps there can be a society where all cultures are recognized and respected. That, then, will be the fulfillment of Teer's vision for the NBT, when America will seem more like "home" to a greater diversity of ethnic groups.

NOTES

1. Barbara Ann Teer, "The Great White Way Is Not Our Way—Not Yet," *Negro Digest*, April 1968, 25.

2. Private Interview March, 1983. National Black Theatre Headquarters

3. Brockett, pp. 384-385.

4. Oscar G. Brockett, *Century of Innovation*, 2nd Ed. (Boston: Allyn and Bacon, 1991), p. 387.

5. Ed Bullins quoted in Marvin X, "An Interview with Ed Bullins," *New Plays From the Black Theatre*, ed. Ed. Bullins (New York: Bantam, 1969), p. xii.

6. Brockett, p. 378.

7. Brockett, p. 399.

8. Hilary Ursula Cohen, *Ritual and Theater: An Examination of Performance Forms in the Contemporary American Theater*, diss., U of Michigan, 1980 (Ann Arbor: UMI, 1980) 167-191.

9. Brockett, p. 378.

10. Teer, p. 28.

11. Oscar G. Brockett, *History of Theatre*, 4th Ed. (Boston: Allyn and Bacon, Inc., 1982), p. 136.

12. John Mbiti, *African Religions and Philosophies* (Garden City, New York: Doubleday Anchor, 1970), p. 73.

13. Mbiti, p. 70.

14. Facts Sheet, National Black Theatre's Healing Hands across Harlem, November 1, 1990, p. 8.

Afterword

Culture is the very foundation on which a people stand. Ethics, values, character and identity all flow from the context of an individual's culture. These values are housed in written narratives, stories, texts and myths which we tell our young. They are taught and instilled in institutions. They are maintained and perpetuated by these institutions for the purpose of molding, shaping and conditioning the way human beings interpret life.

The physical environments in which a person lives and works are colored and shaped by this same cultural context. Human beings at best are only by-products of the physical environments in which they live. The environments that people live in affect their very essence, genes, atoms, thought forms, moods and behavior. Even the nutritional patterns of food consumption are influenced by the environments in which people live. Environments create the moods through which we live our lives, select and wear our clothes, walk, talk, pray, make love, worship, and so forth. In essence, *the sum total of our lifestyle flows from our culture and is reflected in our physical environments as the way we BE in the world.* According to statistics, African American people spent 350 billion dollars on consumer products in 1995, yet the physical environment in which they live is still blighted and is referred to as a "high risk" neighborhood. Why is there not more evidence of this money being circulated in the Black community? Why do the physical environments where Black people live in inner cities all across America reflect such *below level* standards of life and living?

In America, major changes have taken place in Black communities in the social and political arenas. Black people have graduated from a position of having "no rights" to gaining civil rights and from securing civil rights to demanding their human rights. African Americans who have acquired considerable political power are now struggling to gain a foothold on economic power.

We assert that the economic underdevelopment in Black communities is closely related to cultural neglect and cultural blindness. The systematic body of knowledge such as ideas, beliefs, texts and narratives which formulate the stories and myths about our cultural identity are the root cause of our economic crisis. This economic imbalance perpetuates an unsubstantiated public identity, globally, that as a race of people we are inferior, lacking, limited, underdeveloped and undeserving. This assessment is the basis of thought for every Western institution and it must be institutionally corrected and transformed. Furthermore, the inability of Black people to acquire economic empowerment is directly related to the lack of positive cultural and social conditioning, (i. e., the ideas, beliefs, stories and myths) of which we have been taught in school to value, embrace and hold dear.

> "IN THE END, WE CONSERVE WHAT WE LOVE,
> WE LOVE WHAT WE UNDERSTAND AND
> WE UNDERSTAND WHAT WE ARE TAUGHT."

In the American educational institutions, people of African descent have learned to either belittle their cultural contribution, be ashamed of it, take it for granted, avoid it completely or write it off as insignificant. Greater emphasis has been placed on monetary gain, suggesting that more money can be obtained by studying in the fields of Science, Mathematics and Business rather than Blacks studying, understanding, and appreciating the art of their own culture. This blindness and oftentimes pure ignorance of our culture is a major source of the economic underdevelopment of the Black communities across America. We claim that the root cause of the Black experience of poverty and economic underdevelopment in the African American community is a systematic body of knowledge which has resulted from a material reality of "natural scarcity." This reality of thinking and being is a cultural phenomenon of language and is based on an "outside in" interpretation of reality. An "outside in" interpretation is materialistic and finds importance in obtaining "what you see." An "inside out" interpretation is governed by a spiritual base. An energy in believing in "what you don't see."

Culture is the context, the paradigm that holds these ideals, beliefs, stories, texts, myths and narratives in place. Culture as a context of empowerment has been given an extremely low priority among leaders in the Black community. Why are cultural environments so important to the economic viability of a race of people?

As we enter the 21st Century, it is time for the New Village of Harlem to empower its own culture. The word "Harlem" is universal. It is known and recognized worldwide as the Cultural Capital of the Black world. Where are our Cultural Centers, Movie Theaters, Live Theaters, Jazz, Rap or any kind of musical or concert environments? Where are our Lincoln Centers? Where are our sports arenas? Black communities are heavily populated with churches, liquor stores, fast food restaurants and funeral parlors. This physical condition reflects a survival mind set of "eat, sleep, party, get high and die."

The National Black Theatre (NBT) is the first revenue generating Black Theatre Arts Complex and houses the largest collection of new sacred art of the Yoruba culture in the country. Its vision is to develop strong and viable cultural leaders who will bring dignity and autonomy into the communities in which they work, live and serve. These entrepreneurial artists must have a commitment to take care of their own.

We claim that the "Fine Arts" were brought to the earth plane by our African ancestors. They were created for a specific purpose. Their function has always had the mission of furthering the development and growth of human life, and bringing satisfaction, aliveness and joy. Since the context of African culture is rooted in a spiritual reality and not a material reality, the creative power that flows from this spirit culture produces forms of art that energize, educate, awaken, inspire, uplift, and stimulate the imagination. It also entertains the participants while raising their level of consciousness. This creative power generates an intense level of enthusiasm, aliveness, celebration and joy for all who participate.

This inner light which permeates Black art is commonly referred to as "*Soul*." The universal concept of the cultural phenomenon of "*Soul*" is internationally known and associated with the community of Harlem. As stated before, Harlem has long been established as the cultural capital of the Black World and recognized as the soulful home of Black culture. Culture is a context. It is the bowl that holds the artifacts of art. Art is merely the object; it is that something performed or executed by a person or group of people. Art is a skill that must be learned like any other profession. The song, the dance, the performance, the script, and the painting are the consumer products that can be bought or sold in a business exchange and should not be confused with the term culture. Culture cannot be bought or sold!

The Latin root of the word culture is *cultus* which means, "care." Culture means that you will till and tend that for which you care. It is a specific way of thinking and being and is not to be confused with the tangible artifact called art. Strong, economically empowered people *take care of their Culture*. They recognize the intrinsic value of cultural services and products and, therefore, both the culture and the art manifested is heavily endowed financially. Culture is the connecting link to the economic prosperity of a people.

This discourse of culture reflects the narratives, stories, texts, myths, ideas, beliefs, sounds, syllables, words and thought forms of a specific race of people. Culture reflects the histories of institutions and produces all the values and practices unique to a particular group of people. Culturally aware people naturally give back to those things that make them strong.

Culture produces the language which builds character. It produces the thought forms and conversations which generate dignity, trust, unity, respect, and self-love. It produces the images and ideas that mold and shape our public identity. We can therefore no longer blame any outside source for our negative public identity. We must take personal responsibility for the images that the media sends out across the airwaves about who we, as a people, really are. This responsibility lies at the seat of cultural institutions. Black people must build permanent cultural institutions that act as alternate learning environments and that teach people self-love. We speculate that our oppressive plight is a cultural phenomenon of language.

From its inception, The National Black Theatre realized the need to transform the "victim culture" into which Black people were born. Its original purpose was to *maintain and perpetuate the richness and beauty inherent in the form, feeling and force of Black lifestyle.* The National Black Theatre recognizes the need to design, develop and build an alternative culture. One that is prosperous, heroic, inspirational and offers new possibilities.

The major research for the development of "The Reinvention of Black Culture" was discovered in West Africa where I, as the Founder and Chief Executive Officer of the National Black Theatre, realized the cultural phenomenon of African Theatre Art to be an essential and functional element for the human development of people. The art form creates the opportunity for both artists and congregation to create together a healthy and prosperous relationship with their physical environment and the world-at-large.

Since 1968, The National Black Theatre has been producing cultural and artistic products and services that create a balance between the disciplines of business and theatre art. The National Black Theatre has developed hundreds of entrepreneurial artists who have invented the possibility for themselves to live their lives from, day to day, like powerfully poetic works of art.

All of this was made possible out of NBT's commitment to take responsibility for educating and elevating the awareness of people regarding the culture of people of African descent and the importance of NBT's function toward the liberation of its people from old beliefs and attitudes that produce below level standards of living. Its mission is one that demands first the development of human beings. In the beginning, the courses address the question "what does it mean to be human?" in a profound and creative way. A creative process was invented that is rooted in a spiritual culture and designed from a love centered base. The course where this creative process is taught is called *"TEER, The Technology of Soul."*

This love centered philosophy is not only inspiring and uplifting, but it is also a powerful tool for economic development. It has guided the development of an Entrepreneurial Artist Program. NBT's cultural context has allowed NBT to successfully bridge the gap between business and art. Thus, the NBT embraces the new name of *The National Black Theatre's Institute of Action Arts* indicating such growth.

In honor of this change and our many accomplishments, the city of New York has changed the local law to rename the streets intersecting at The National Black Theatre. 125th Street was changed to Fredrica L. Teer Square, after my sister the late Executive Director of the National Black Theatre. She was an inspirational force for us all. Fifth Avenue has been renamed National Black Theatre Way.

Dr. Barbara Ann Teer

Appendices

Appendix A

THE RITUAL: TO REGAIN OUR STRENGTH AND RECLAIM OUR POWER

In 1970, the NBT premiered *The Ritual: To Regain Our Strength and Reclaim Our Power*. In May, 1971, Thomas Johnson, a critic for the *New York Times*, provided an outline of the revival's tone and action:

A young woman enters singing "Sometimes I feel Like a Motherless Child" as Barbara Ann Teer appears in a floor- length, fire orange robe with gold-plated breastplate stating, "Yes, Black people, we are a long way from home. We've been on a bad trip. Now together, let us take this spiritual journey—we're coming home." Thirty liberators come from different directions to the stage area where Teer is located in a "Theatre in the round" space. The liberators appear to be actors, dancers, and singers all at once. The music begins to pick up a faster beat as the liberators began to chant, "Set free, Set free." As they continue to chant, Teer states over the chanting, "The power is in me, We're going home now." The liberators move through the audience keeping rhythms with drums, chanting, "We need you, we want you. Got to have you, we are you." Then a series of dramatic and musical scenes followed which depicted the problems and frustrations of urban Black Americans. Intertwined with the scenes, liberators urge—"[t]ake a good look at your mind." A young girl begins to shout, "[w]ake up, wake up—make your own magic. Don't wait for it to happen. You are magic." Quickly the street scene becomes a church scene and a dancing liberator who was feeling good was urged by others to "testify brother, testify." The testifying liberator states, "I do believe I can feel the fire, I do believe that I am that fire. I do believe I can reclaim that power." The ritual ended with a revival-like finale—with both liberators and audience members together in the performing space dancing, clapping hands, and singing together, "We are an African people, together we can change this mixed-up land." [1]

Appendix B

A REVIVAL: CHANGE/LOVE TOGETHER/ORGANIZE!

In July of 1972, *A Revival: Change/ Love Together/ Organize!* was conceived by Teer, who also directed the play. Written by Charlie Russell, also playwright of *The Believers* which Teer had directed in 1968, *A Revival* unfolded, according to Jessica Harris, as follows:

> As you enter the first space, the liberators casually show you to a seat and talk to you about various things, or try to panhandle, or dance. This action takes place in the street setting. This continues until the main story begins: Porky, a junkie, owes money to Walt, a pusher, but he has lost the money and cannot pay. He resorts to stealing a woman's wallet but is caught. So he has no way to return the money that he owes Walt. When Walt comes to town, he threatens Porky and gives him a short time to come up with the money. In his flight from Walt, Porky has been befriended by Toussaint, who is the leader of the Temple of Liberation. Toussaint invites all the liberators and spectators to attend a revival later in the evening. This action is juxtaposed with the descent of the goddess Oshun, Yoruba goddess of Love. Oshun sees what has happened to her children, sees the state of the community, and exhorts all to unify and love each other. The descent of Oshun is the occasion for a scene of possession taken from the voodoo rites of Haiti and is one of the highpoints [*sic*] of the first part of the performance. Another highpoint is a fire dance that marks the entrance of the Kabakas, who present the revival in the second part of the performance. . . . A wall of the space is then rolled back, and the spectators are ushered under a heavy chain and into the Temple of Liberation. The atmosphere of the temple is completely different from that of the street. It is spiritual and not worldly. Most of the spectators are surprised to see the characters from the first part

of the piece in the temple. But the plot continues. The first few minutes in the temple are spent introducing the Kabakas, the Liberators, and ourselves. Information gleaned from a book tells the spectators that blacks form only 11 percent of the population of the United States but that they drink more than 49 percent of the scotch consumed in the country and 25 percent of the grape soda; they spend 200-million dollars on suits and 8-million dollars on ties. The Kabakas feed the audience this information and then tell the spectators that blacks have money and power to support black institutions—not only the Temple of Liberation but all black institutions. The audience becomes so caught up in this that when the plot continues—Walt breaks into the temple to look for Porky—it seems to be an intrusion. . . . Walt takes Porky from the temple. Sometime later, Porky is returned to the temple, but he has been brutally beaten by Walt. This is the occasion for a scene of healing in the manner of the faith-healing evangelists. Toussaint, the leader of the Kabakas, heals Porky and implores him not to go back to dope and the life of the streets but rather to become a spiritual being and to work for positive black change.[2]

Appendix C
SOLJOURNEY INTO TRUTH

Soljourney into Truth was created and directed by Teer in 1974. According to Larry Conley, a reviewer for the Columbia University "City Scope," *Soljourney* began with a conversation between the liberators and members of the audience:

"Hi, my name is Ayodele, I'm your flight attendant for tonight. And you're (glancing at the name tag) . . . Larry. Larry, how do you feel about someone you don't know coming up and talking to you?"

"Well, I don't know. It's kind of strange,"

"Uh-huh. Do you like to travel?"

"Sure, who doesn't?"

"Oh, you're so right. What is it that you like about traveling?"

"Not having to work."

She laughs. "Well, do you have any idea about what to expect from this evening?"

"No, not really."

"We're going to hold hands, sing, and get a chance to feel good inside. Would you like that?"

"Uhhh, I guess so."

"Good! Larry, I'm really glad to see you here tonight, and I hope you enjoy the evening."

"Oh, I expect to."

"Take care." And then she's off to greet another new arrival.

"Hi, my name is Ayodele . . ."

. . . Next Adeyemi comes forth stating I'm one of your flight captains for tonight's "Soljourney into Truth" . . . and asks the audience members to shout out their biggest problem and the audience responds. He then assures them all that before the evening is over they will discover a way to solve their problems, by getting away from those "oppressive belief systems" that prevail in this world, which he calls the "Land of Not." . . . Later he asks the audience to get up and circulate, introducing themselves to one another. Suddenly, while the audience is engaged in this process, the lights go out and music begins booming from all sides. The audience is whisked into another large room, known as the Liberation Temple. Two female liberators join together in an engaging song about discovering "the real you"; a male performer enacts a gospel-like routine about exorcising fear and inhibition; another performer delivers an emotional soliloquy about the ways in which black people have been geared to "expect less, say no, and refrain from hoping." There is also a lot of speculation about the secret ingredient needed to propel the "sunship" into the heavens—an ingredient later revealed to be love. Then, in the form of a fantastic African ritual, the so-called ship "takes off." Adeyemi, with a feathered headdress and African garb, appears as a chieftain to whom gifts are brought. Dancers twirl and even manage some ballet-like pirouettes and leaps. Warbles and chants sound in the background. Psychedelic lights flash eerily across the scene. As the calm returns to the theater, Teer descends from her throne. "We're really up there now. Don't look down if you're scared of heights." ... At her urging everyone chooses a partner and takes turns singing the NBT song: "You're the only one who can make yourself happy. You're the only one who can fill your life with joy." Teer instructs the members of the audience to close their eyes and think about their first love, about themselves, and about the kind of person they would like to become. ... Finally, in a move reminiscent of an old-fashioned gospel revival, Teer asks for testimonials from the audience. One young white male gets up and fumbles for words. "Wow!" I'm just glad to be here." A black teacher rises and talks about getting his "love cup filled here tonight." A teenage girl comes forward shyly: "I'm really bashful. But I feel so good, I wish it would never end." One young mother comes to the front and, in a sincere, quiet voice, says that the performance has reinforced her love for her husband.[3]

Appendix D
SOFTLY COMES A WHIRLWIND WHISPERING IN YOUR EAR

In 1978, Teer wrote *Softly Comes a Whirlwind Whispering in Your Ear*, "based on the real life story of its star, Zuri McKie."[4] The play treated a young lady, her relationship with family and friends, as well as her talent for singing. Betty Winston Baye described the main character and her circumstances:

> The success of *Whirlwind* lies in Ms. McKie's ability to make the audience relate to and identify with her struggles as a middle- class young Black woman ... her mother's almost fanatical drive to make her a great singer, not unlike Leontyne Price, and the pain she feels pursuing a master's degree in opera and piano while her father languishes in prison for a crime he did not commit. Ms. McKie makes one identify with her decision to break with her mother—she doesn't talk to her for three years—and doesn't want her mother to come to

hear her sing in a benefit to raise money for her father's release. "I don't want my mother and all her bourgeoisie friends to come," Ms. McKie says. We watch Ms. McKie struggle to get free of her own private prison—the one that has locked her up emotionally, but which is hidden under the veneer of "having it all together."[5]

Amy Carter, writing for the *Bilanian News* continues with information on Iansa, her father, and her friends:

The play . . . depicts Iansa Colburn, a young lady who intends to get her father out of jail with money earned by singing in a concert. She intends the concert to be just a one- shot deal but her friend, Ajire, played by Keibu Faison, wants her to go on to bigger things. Iansa . . . protests against Ajire's ambitions for her and points out that among other things, she will not be packaged and sold like a can of beans. However, her friends Benny and Sonya Michaels tell Iansa that music and songs don't have to be sex-oriented and an insult to the human intelligence. They advise her that music can be used to inspire, to bring peace, love and understanding between people. Then, Iansa decides to pursue a singing career.[6]

Appendix E
SOUL FUSION

The fifth major ritual performed by the NBT was *Soul Fusion*, written by Nabii Faison and Teer in collaboration with Leone Thomas in 1980. *Soul Fusion* had a more traditional plot than *Whirlwind* but its message took the form of one or two-lined inspirational passages, such as these:

Get in touch with your dream. . . . Love ain't love until you give it away. . . . This theater can be that place where we can feel strong again. You are the source of that power. . . . There's a fusion, a connection when the performer and the audience come together. . . . It's time to commit ourselves to each other.[7]

Yusef Salaam hints that the revival "might be alluding to the closing of the Apollo Theatre and the economic blight of Harlem."[8] He summarizes the plot as follows:

> The story involves Jack Henry Bruwell (Tunde Samuel), who is the director of the Old Theatre in Harlem; the theatre lights are being cut off by Con Edison at a time when the cast is working on a major production. . . . Jack is a hopeless pessimist. He gives up all hope of saving this theatre. But his woman friend and his cast challenge him to dare to struggle. They remind him of the vim and vigor days of the Old Theatre when James Brown, Aretha Franklin and Dinah Washington graced its stage. Rebecca Branch (Shirley Faison), Jack's woman friend, demands that he be self-reliant and seek independent ownership of the institution. She believes that these attributes will, if practiced, save the theatre from its desperate plight. But Jack remains welded in his negative, failure-prone attitude until he's visited by masked, colorfully costumed characters; some of them positive forces, some negative. The negative ones call out for Jack to "Get a real job and leave that theatre be" while the positives demand that he see the light. Here, witness audio-visual psychic and emotional dynamite. Jack struggles to purge himself of the psychological garbage that society has dumped in him. . . . As Jack ventures into the realm of faith, self confidence, and belief in himself and his community, he sees the light, internalizes it. It's revealed that one of the cast members has a friend who works at Con Edison, and she can use her connections to keep the theatre lights connected. Inspired, Jack, the cast and Benny Jackson (a famous star who returns to Harlem to help revitalize it) put on a show that had even the senior citizens swinging. Somebody jumped up and declared, "I want to see a 500-seat theatre in Harlem."[9]

Appendix F
THE LEGACY

The Legacy was a musical written by Gordon Nelson, a graduate of NBT's The Power in You Writer's Workshop. Elmo Terry-Morgan, a graduate of the Teer Technology of Soul class, directed the fourteen-member cast in this gospel musical. Joyce Ashe, of the *Rockaway Press* wrote that

> "The Legacy" is a musical that traces the history of gospel music from the African shores to the slave plantations, through emancipation, the civil rights movement and the present time. It is serious theatre, although it is the story of a genre of music, and music is generally associated with entertainment. One learns . . . that gospel music and the unswerving faith that it expresses sustained the Black people through centuries of slavery, poverty, misery and oppression. . . . "The Legacy" is narrated by a majestic figure swarthed in flaming orange African robes, who is called "The Ancestor." He represents the ancestral leader, the village chief, and the African concept of the "Father/God." He assures his people that He is with them, always, through their trials, throughout the Diaspora. His spirit is indelibly and forever imprinted in their hearts and in their blood, in their genetic heritage. He speaks to His people through the music. The finale is the statement: ". . . Let nothing separate us from the love of God." The gospel music expresses the determination of the Black people to resist attack, their power to rise up, and "sing like a holy army." The Ancestor says, "We have been riding on the River Gospel, our faith has sustained us, 'til we find ourselves home."[10]

NOTES TO APPENDIX

1. Johnson, E-44.
2. Jessica B. Harris, 288-291.

3. Larry Conley, "NBT: Theatre of Soul," *City Scope* (New York: Journal of Columbia University, 1976), 53.

4. Betty Winston Baye, "'Softly Comes the Whirlwind' ushers in Spring at NBT" *NY Amsterdam News* 10 May 1980, 32.

5. Baye, 32.

6. Amy Carter, "'Softly Comes a Whirlwind Whispering in Your Ears'" *Bilalian News* 13 June 1980, 24., col. 1-2.

7. R[oy] P[roctor], "'Soul Fusion' is New Approach to Theatre," *Richmond News Leader* 1 November 1982, 15.

8. Yusef A. Salaam, "'Soul Fusion' Inspires Community Control thro' Community Theatre," *NY Amsterdam News* 12 June 1982, 36.

9. Salaam, 36.

10. Joyce Ashe, "'The Legacy'—An Unforgettable Night," *Rockaway Press*, 17 December 1987, vol. 3, no. 49, 24.

Appendix H
HANDOUT FROM TEER ON FREEDOM
Freedom

To be free means that you are autonomous. Working at your "CONFIDENCE CENTER" for at least 15 minutes each day will free you of old stressful angers and hostilities and your inner resignation and rage. We invite you to experience a mood of peace. Peace is a conversation without worry or doubt.

Learn to stop taking your relational cues from the outside world. Begin taking all your cues from the "heart." Ask yourself the questions: What do I care about? What are my concerns? What is my commitment?

Begin to respond to the outside world instant by instant, free of any dictates from the world out there. Shift your conversations. Move through your life from the conversation of "COMMITMENT."

Most people determine their lives by their circumstances. Your circumstances usually determine your response. American culture breeds us to react to our outside circumstances and so when we are in misery, pain and unhappiness, we try to change the outside circumstances because we think we are determined by that context. For centuries Americans have tried to change their outside world to escape their inner pain. They see themselves separate from their so called Reality.

Who we are is a conversation. We are connected to that conversation in our bodyhood and in our listening.

In this course, we want to reconnect you back to a conversation of the heart. We encourage you to find your commitment in life. What turns you on, what you care about. Over the years, this connection has been broken. We encourage you to take your cues from the heart, from your Being and as a result not to be determined by your circumstances out there.

People who are determined by their circumstances and who are reacting in anger are ineffective in what they are trying to do. As long as you are determined by the circumstance, you can't, you can't change that circumstance. All you are doing is reflecting on it. You are simply replicating it. If you operate from your commitment, from your heart, from your concerns and caring, you immediately become effective in the world. Speak and listen from your Commitment.

We all have a great longing to become Whole, Complete, Self Confident and Holy. When you operate from the heart, this begins to happen. Commitment moves things, Makes things happen. In getting in touch with your commitment, life becomes exciting. Life becomes peaceful and joyous. God is not something separate and outside of you. God is an omnipresence, a divine intelligence happening in a specific type of conversation going on always in your listening.

CONVERSATION FOR CONFIDENCE CENTER

You are the Self. You are of God. God's power within you is greater than any challenge or circumstances of the world. You are stronger than any negative influence in your life. No habit, no life-style, no personality has the power over you to block your full expression of the health, prosperity, wisdom, peace and joy.

The Spirit, The Self, the I AM is great within you. It is a divine intelligence, a Conversation!

NBT is your permanent Home away from Home! Join this family, it is your family. Stay in touch with the Power within. Reinvent your identity, Redesign your Self. Thank you for joining this Course!

Barbara Ann Teer

Bibliography

BOOKS AND ANTHOLOGIES

Anderson, James A. "Cognitive Styles and Multicultural Populations." Journal of Teacher Education. Jan.-Feb. 1988.

Banks, James A. *Teaching Strategies for Ethnic Studies*. 5th Ed. Boston: Allyn and Bacon, 1971

Baraka, Amiri, *Blues People: Negro Music in White America*. New York: William Morrow, 1963.

Beier, Ulli. *The Sacred Art of Susanne Wenger*. London: Cambridge UP, 1975.

Bennett, Jr., Lerone. *Before the Mayflower: A History of Black America*. 5th Ed. Chicago: Johnson, 1982.

Brockett, Oscar. *Century of Innovation*. 2nd ed. Boston: Allyn and Bacon, 1991.

———. *History of the Theatre*. 4th ed. Boston: Allyn and Bacon, 1982.

Brown, Clifton F. "Black Religion—1968." *In Black America*. Los Angeles: Presidential Publishers, 1970.

Calley, Malcolm J. C. *God's People: West Indian Pentecostal Sects in England*. London: Cambridge UP, 1965.

Cohen, Hilary Ursula. *Ritual and Theater: An Examination of Performance Forms in the Contemporary American Theater*. Diss. U of Michigan, 1980.

Davis, Ossie. "The Flight from Broadway." *Negro Digest* April 1966.

Dee, Ruby. "The Tattered Queens." *The International Library of Negro Life and History-Anthology of the American Negro in the Theatre*. 2nd ed. Ed. Lindsay Patterson. New York: Publisher's, 1969.

Drewal, Henry John and Margaret Thompson Drewal. *Gelede: Art and Power Among the Yoruba*. Bloomington, Indiana UP, 1983.

Dunbar, Paul Lawrence. "We Wear the Mask." *Black Voices: An Anthology of Afro-American Literature*. Ed. Abraham Chapman. New York: New American Library, 1968.

Fabre, Genevieve. *Drumbeats, Masks, and Metaphor*. Trans. Melvin Dixon. Cambridge: Harvard UP, 1983.

Harris, Jessica B. "The National Black Theatre: The Sun People of 125th Street." Ed. Errol Hill *The Theatre of Black Americans*. New York: Applause, 1987.

Harris, Valerie. "Power Exchange 2: Barbara Ann Teer." *Third World Women: The Politics of Being Other*. Vol. 2. New York: Heresies Collective, 1979.

Haskins, James. *Black Theater in America*. New York: Crowell, 1982.

Hatch, James V. "Here Comes Everybody: Scholarship and Black Theatre History." *Interpreting the Theatrical Past: Essays in Historiography of Performance*. Eds. Thomas Postlewait and Bruce McConachie. Iowa City: U of Iowa P, 1989.

———. *Black Theatre U.S.A.* Cons. Ted shine. New York: Free Press, 1974.

———. "Some African Influences on the Afro-American Theatre." Ed. *The Theatre of Black Americans*. Ed. Errol Hill New York: Applause, 1987.

Herskovits, Melville J. *The Myth of the Negro Past*. New York: Harper and Brothers, 1940.

Hollenweger, W. J. *The Pentecostals: The Charismatic Movement in the Churches*. Minneapolis: Augsburg, 1972.

Holy Bible, King James Version. Nashville: Holman Bible Publishers, 1979.

Hughes, Langston. "The Need for an Afro-American Theatre." *The International Library of Negro Life and History-Anthology of the American Negro in the Theatre*. 2nd Ed. Ed. Lindsay Patterson. New York: Publisher's, 1969.

Isaacs, Edith. *The Negro in the American Theatre*. New York: Theatre Arts, 1947.

Jeyifous, Abiodun. "Black Critics on Black Theatre in America." *The Black Theatre in America*. Ed. Errol Hill. New York: Applause, 1987.

King, Jr., Woodie and Ron Milner, Eds. *Black Drama Anthology*. New York: New American Library, 1971.

King, Jr., Woodie. "Problems Facing Negro Actors," T*he International Library of Negro Life and History-Anthology of the American Negro in the Theatre*. 2nd Ed. Ed. Lindsay Patterson. New York: Publishers Company, 1969.

Levine, Mindy N. *New York's Other Theatre: A Guide to Off Off Broadway*. New York: Avon Books, 1981.

Mapp, Edward. "Teer, Barbara Ann." *Directory of Blacks in the Performing Arts*. Metuchen: Scarecrow Press, 1978.

Matney, William C. "Teer, Barbara Ann." *Who's Who Among Black Americans, Inc.* 1st Ed. Northbrook: Publishing, 1976.

Mbiti, John. *African Religions and Philosophies*. Garden City, New York: Doubleday Anchor, 1970.

McConachie, Bruce. "Using the Concept of Cultural Hegemony to Write Theatre History." *Interpreting the Theatrical Past: Essays in Historiography of Performance*. Eds. Thomas Postlewait and Bruce McConachie. Iowa City: U of Iowa P, 1989.

Mitchell, Loften. *Black Drama: The Story of the American Negro in the Theatre*. New York: Hawthorn, 1967.

Neal, Larry. "The Black Art Movement." *The Drama Review*. Summer 1968.

———. "Into Nationalism, Out of Parochialism." *The Theatre of Black Americans*. Ed. Errol Hill. New York: Applause, 1987.

Peterson, Jr., Bernard L. *Contemporary Black American Playwrights and Their Plays: A Biographical Directory and Dramatic Index*. Westport: Greenwood Press, 1988.

Ploski, Harry and Ernest Kaiser. Eds. "The Constitution of the United States." *Afro USA*. New York: Bellwether Publishing, 1971.

Ploski, Harry and James Williams. Eds. "The Black Entertainer in the Performing Arts." *The Negro Almanac*. New York: John Wiley and Sons, 1983.

"Primus, Pearl." *Current Biography: Who's News and Why 1944*. New York: H. W. Wilson Co., 1945.

Sanders, Leslie. *The Development of Black Theatre: From Shadows to Selves*. Baton Rouge: Louisiana State UP, 1988.

Shange, Ntozake. *Spell #7. 9 Plays by Black Women.* Ed. Margaret Wilkerson. New York: New American Library, 1986.

"Soul." *Merriam-Webster Dictionary, The.* New York: Pocket Books, 1974.

Teer, Barbara Ann. "The Great white Way is Not Our Way—Not Yet." *Negro Digest* April 1968.

Troyka, Lynn Quitman. *The Simon and Shuster Handbook for Writers,* 2nd ed. Englewood Cliffs: Prentice-Hall, 1990.

Walker, Ethel Pitts. "The American Negro Theatre." *The Theatre of Black Americans* Ed. Errol Hill. New York: Applause, 1987.

Walton, Ortiz M. "A Comparative Analysis of the African and the Western Aesthetics." *The Black Aesthetic.* Ed. Addison Gayle, Jr., New York: Doubleday, 1971.

Wenger, Susanne. *The Timeless Mind of the Sacred: Its New Manifestation in the Osun Grove.* Oshogbo: Adeyemi Press, 1977.

Wilkerson, Margaret. "Critics, Standards and Black Theatre." *The Theatre of Black Americans.* Ed. Errol Hill. New York: Applause, 1987.

Williams, Mance. *Black Theatre in the 1960s and 1970s: A Historical-Critical Analysis of the Movement.* Westport: Greenwood, 1985.

Wilson, Edwin. *The Theater Experience.* 5th Ed. New York: McGraw-Hill, 1991.

X, Marvin. "An Interview with Ed Bullins: Black Theatre." *Negro Digest* April 1969.

JOURNALS AND MAGAZINES

"Accent on New Possibilities." NBT Magazine 1 Spring-Summer, 1987: 1-12.

"Barbara Ann Teer and The National Black Theatre." *Interreligious Foundation for Community Organization News* Jan.-Feb. 1972: 1.

"Barbara Ann Teer: Producer." *Ebony* 32 Aug. 1977:138.

Beckmann, David M. "Trance from Africa to Pentecostalism." *Concordia Theological Monthly.* 45 Jan. 1974.

Clark, William A. "Sanctification in Negro Religion." *Social Forces* 5 May 1937: 547-48.

Cotto-Escalera, Brenda L. "Masks, Performance Traditions, and Cultural Diversity: Exploring African Culture through African Masks." *Theatre and Education Youth Theatre Journal* (1991):10-12.

DuBois, William E. B. "The Little Krigwa Players," *Crisis Magazine*. 32 July, 1926: 133-34.

———. "The Negro Art." *Crisis Magazine*. 32 Oct. 1926: 290-96.

Guiden, Antoine T. "The Vision of Barbara Ann Teer." *AUDELCO's Overture Magazine*. Winter, 1984-85: n. pag.

Hollenweger, Walter J. "Pentecostalism and Black Power." *Theology Today* 30 Oct. 1973: 231-237.

Jones, Martha M. "Barbara Ann Teer's National Black Theatre." *Black Creation* 3 Summer 1972: 19-23.

Lovett, Reverand Leonard. "The Spiritual Legacy and Role of Black Holiness-Pentecostalism in the Development of American Culture." *One in Christ* 23 (1987): 149.

McConachie, Bruce. "Towards a Postpositivist Theatre History." *Theatre Journal* 37 (1985): 474-75.

Myers, Linda James. "The Nature of Pluralism and the African American Case." *Theory into Practice*. 20(1981): 1-6.

Patterson, Lindsay. "The National Black Theater Thrives." *Theatreweek* 28 Mar. 1988: 31.

Porter, Curtiss E. "THIS HERE CHILD IS NAKED AND FREE AS A BIRD: AN ANNOTATED INTERVIEW WITH BARBARA ANN TEER." *Black Lines*. 2 Spring 1973: 15-32.

Russell, Charlie L. "Barbara Ann Teer: We Are Liberators Not Actors." *Essence* Mar. 1971: 48-52.

Simpson, George Eaton. "Black Pentecostalism in the United States." *Phylon* 35 (1987): 200-10.

Tinney, James S. "Black Origins of the Pentecostal Movement." *Christianity Today* 8 Oct. 1971: 1-7.

Williams, Robert C. "Ritual, Drama, and God in Black Religion: Theological and Anthropological Views." *Theology Today* 41 Jan. 1985: 433-36.

NEWSPAPER CITATIONS

Allsopp, Clarence. "The National Black Theatre Gets Set to Revive Harlem."
   NY Amsterdam News 22 July 1972: D-3.
Ashe, Joyce. "'The Legacy' - An Unforgettable Night." *Rockaway Press* 17
   Dec. 1987: 24.
Baye, Betty Winston. "'Softly Comes a Whirlwind' ushers in Spring at NBT."
   NY Amsterdam News 10 May 1980: 32.
Berry, Kelly-Marie. "The Legacy: Memories of the Gospel Song." *Metro
   Exchange.* Aug. 1987: 11.
Best, Tony. "Barbara Ann Teer and the Liberators." *NY Amsterdam News* 12
   Nov. 1975: D-10.
Bivins, Larry. "Success Without Compromise." *Newsday* 14 Apr. 1988: 24.
"Black Theatre Breaks Ground." *The Philadelphia Tribune* 16 May 1989: C-1.
Burden, Charles. "'Whirlwind' is Not Just a Play, It's a Happening." *NY News
   World.* 2 May 1980: 27.
Burden, Charles. "A Trip to Africa Brings Hope to America." *NY News World*
   2 June 1980: 2B.
"Daddy Rice." *New York Times* 5 June 1881: 32.
Davis, Curt. "Drama Reviews: Softly Comes a Whirlwind— Whispering in
   Your Ear." *Other Stages* 17 Apr. 1980:
DeLeon, Albert. "Can There Be A Revival?" *The Black American* 11 Sept.,
   1972: 11.
Givens II, Michael C. "Soljourney Takes Off at Beacon Theatre." *N Y
   Amsterdam News* 19 May 1979: 34.
Hazziezah. "NBT's 'Ritual' to Awaken 'Sun People,'" *NY Amsterdam News* 12
   Nov. 1977: D-9.
Husar, Ruth. "She Celebrates the Black Life-Style." *Bridgeport Post* 9 Aug.
   1974: n. pag.
Johnson, Thomas A. "On Harlem Stage, A Spiritual Journey." *New York Times*
   11 May 1971: E-44.
Kawe. "International Cooperation in Drama." *Sunday Sketch* 9 Sept. 1973: 1.
M. S. *CUC* 2 Dec. 1972.
Mauby. "A Powerful Journey into Truth." *Trinidad Guardian* 18 Dec. 1975: 1.
Mitchell, Lionel H. "NBT Scores with Whirlwind." *NY Amsterdam News* 6 Jan.
   1979: 15.

"NBT Conducts Workshop Series." *NY Amsterdam News* 19 June 1976: D-14.

"NBT Offers Performing Writers Workshop." *NY Amsterdam News* 1 Mar. 1986: 25.

"NBT Workshops in Creative Energy." *NY Amsterdam News* 9 October 1976: D-8.

"NBT Opens New Season." *NY Amsterdam News* 12 Nov. 1977: D- 14.

Peterson, Maurice. "Spotlight on Barbara Ann Teer." *Essence* Aug. 1975:19.

P[roctor], R[oy]. "'Soul Fusion' is New Approach to Theater." *Richmond News Leader* 1 Nov. 1982: 15.

Riley, Clayton. "Face to Face With the Junkies." *New York Times* 17 Sept. 1972:

Salaam, Yusef A. "'Soul Fusion' Inspires Community Control thro' Community Theatre." *NY Amsterdam News* 12 June 1982: 36.

Satterwhite, Sandy. "Black Actress Shares Her Soul." *New York Post* 6 Feb. 1976:21.

Schoichet, Gary. "Barbara Ann Teer." *Other Stages* 17 Apr. 1980: 2.

Teer, Barbara Ann. "Reinvention of a people." *NY Amsterdam News* 22 Dec. 1984:13.

CLASSES AND INTERVIEWS

Faison, Ade. Personal interview. 25 June 1992.

"The Issue is Race." Mod. Phil Donahue. *MacNeil/Lehrer News Hour*. PBS. WNET, New York. 15 Sept. 1991.

O'Brien, Michael. Personal Interview. 17 Dec. 1992.

Samuel, Tunde. Personal Interview. 24 June 1992.

Teer, Barbara Ann. Personal Interview. 26 Feb. 1983.

Teer, Barbara Ann. Telephone Interview. 19 Mar. 1986.

Teer, Barbara Ann. Personal Interview. 23 Oct. 1987.

Teer, Barbara Ann. "Identity, Dignity, and Trust Class." Harlem, 24 Oct. 1987.

Teer, Barbara Ann. Teer Technology of Soul II Class. Harlem, 20 Jan. 1988.

Teer, Barbara Ann. Personal Interview. 21 July 1992.

PAMPHLETS AT NATIONAL BLACK THEATRE HEADQUARTERS

Facts Sheet. National Black Theatre's Healing Hands Across Harlem. 1 Nov. 1990.

Faison, Abisola. Teer Technology of Soul Workshops Advertising Pamphlet, 1985.

National Black Theatre Newsletter. 1 Nov. 1986: 1-4. NBT is a Celebration of Life and a Rebirth of Power. 1973: 1-6.

Teer, Barbara Ann. "Freedom." Hand Out Sheet for Entrepreneurial Class, 1987.

Teer, Barbara Ann. "The National Black Theatre's Institute of Action Arts." *The Legacy* Tour USA 1989 Pamphlet, 1987.

"The National Black Theatre Milestones." Publicity Material from the National Black Theatre, 1983.

Index